MW01030661

PRAISE FOR *OUTGROW*

"Alex Goldfayn has been instrumental in transforming our company's approach to sales. His guidance in implementing an Outgrow proactive sales culture has been the catalyst for our incredible growth, doubling our revenue over the past three years. By encouraging consistent communication with clients and fostering a mindset of outreach and relationship-building, Alex has empowered our sales team to perform at a higher level. His strategies have instilled confidence, accountability, and focus throughout the organization, driving results far beyond our expectations. We couldn't have achieved this level of success without his expertise and commitment to our success."
—Michael Meiresonne, Chief Operating Officer, DSG Supply

"*Outgrow* has helped our company and engineers get beyond the fear of 'selling' and understand they already have the abilities to help their clients more—they just need to take deliberate proactive action and ask *How can we help?* This is at the core of an Outgrow company: We're not selling; we're helping. And now, our people believe this!"
—Molly E. Foley, Principal and Chief Marketing Officer, IMEG Corp.

"Alex Goldfayn's *Outgrow* is a simple methodology of growing sales organically, which has reaped massive rewards for our business. His program has become ingrained in our culture of proactive service to our customers and business partners."
—Taylor Tankersley, Vice President, East Coast Lumber

"Alex Goldfayn has turned into a friend and been instrumental in how we think about selling and revenue. I didn't realize we could turn all our customer-facing employees into revenue generators. *Outgrow* has been a game changer for our company."
—Michael Gianni, Founder and CEO, MD7

"Alex Goldfayn is unapologetically candid in his desire to help leaders adjust their mindsets toward being intentional in their everyday sales approach. His simple Outgrow strategies are effective and time efficient. *Outgrow* brings us a set of tools that even non-sales people can adopt and find long term success with."
—Curt Williams, Principal/Director, I.C. Thomasson

"*Outgrow* has allowed our team to shine bright in our customers' eyes. The Outgrow proactive actions we implement save our customers time and money and ultimately make our business grow for the long haul."
—Brent Jones, Vice President, J&B Supply, Inc.

"*Outgrow* has helped our company focus on a selling approach that helps a 'non-sales person' become a proactive seller and not just an order taker."
—Matt Hasselbring, Pricing Manager, Ace Supply

"*Outgrow* has helped our company install rigor around our selling process to achieve long-term measurable results. I would recommend Alex and his Outgrow selling tools to help drive sales at your organization."

—Robert Davidson, Chief Executive Officer, Alexander Chemical Corp.

"*Outgrow* is helping us systemize our way of building relationships with our clients as we scale our business."

—Stephen Coulthard, Chief Business Officer, Cumming Group

"*Outgrow* has significantly helped our company by empowering engineers at all levels to confidently and proactively sell to both new and existing clients. This approach has not only boosted our sales but also enhanced our team's overall confidence and effectiveness in client interactions."

—Phillip Sutherland, Principal, I.C. Thomasson Associates, Inc.

"Alex Goldfayn's Outgrow process has allowed Cumming Group the ability to stay focused on our clients, and, as a result, supercharged revenue generation through our team members' existing relationships."

—Thomas Noto, Vice President Business Development, Cumming Group

"Outgrow has transformed our sales platform by making it structured and scalable. The added benefit is that it's a lot of fun!"

—Gus Childs, Owner, City Supply

"*Outgrow* has helped UCC grow by implementing the most simple techniques, tools, and processes with a systematic disciplined approach. This was accomplished through elevated visibility that accelerates personal motivation in a fun manner!"

—Andrew Matthews, Vice President of Sales, Americas, UCC Environmental

"*Outgrow* has helped our company exceed our industry's expected growth. The tools, strategies, and techniques are something any sales organization can implement and succeed with."

—Joe Solheid, Vice President, Sales and Marketing, DSG Supply

"Outgrow is a structured approach to sales that tracks measurable actions that lead to real sales growth. No more sales people throwing spaghetti against a wall or using a shotgun approach with their customers!"

—Chris Fairchild, Vice President, Sales and Marketing, Alexander Chemical Corp.

ALSO BY ALEX GOLDFAYN

Pick Up the Phone and Sell
5-Minute Selling
Selling Boldly
The Revenue Growth Habit
Evangelist Marketing

OUTGROW

How to Expand Market Share and Outsell Your Competition

ALEX GOLDFAYN

Matt Holt Books
An Imprint of BenBella Books, Inc.
Dallas, TX

This book is designed to provide accurate and authoritative information about sales. Neither the author nor the publisher is engaged in rendering legal, accounting, or other professional services by publishing this book. If any such assistance is required, the services of qualified professionals should be sought. The author and publisher will not be responsible for any liability, loss, or risk incurred as a result of the use and application of any information contained in this book.

Outgrow copyright © 2025 by Alex Goldfayn

All rights reserved.Except in the case of brief quotations embodied in critical articles or reviews, no part of this book may be used or reproduced, stored, transmitted, or used in any manner whatsoever, including for training artificial intelligence (AI) technologies or for automated text and data mining, without prior written permission from the publisher.

Matt Holt is an imprint of BenBella Books, Inc.
8080 N. Central Expressway
Suite 1700
Dallas, TX 75206
benbellabooks.com
Send feedback to feedback@benbellabooks.com

BenBella and *Matt Holt* are federally registered trademarks.

Printed in the United States of America
10 9 8 7 6 5 4 3 2 1

Library of Congress Control Number: 2024045345
ISBN 9781637746394 (hardcover)
ISBN 9781637746400 (electronic)

Editing by Katie Dickman
Copyediting by Michael Fedison
Proofreading by Lisa Story and Marissa Wold Uhrina
Indexing by WordCo Indexing Services, Inc.
Text design and composition by Aaron Edmiston
Cover design by Brigid Pearson
Printed by Lake Book Manufacturing

Special discounts for bulk sales are available.
Please contact bulkorders@benbellabooks.com.

To Lisa
Two kids. Four homes. Six dogs. Seven books.
Thank you for your relentless belief.

CONTENTS

Outgrow is . . .

Systematically and proactively expanding
your business with customers and prospects,
especially those you don't talk with regularly.

Which is most of them.

WHAT IS OUTGROW?

I n one sentence, Outgrow is a trackable, measurable system for growing your business by: (1) consistently expanding your wallet share with current customers, and (2) proactively communicating with the many customers and prospects who you don't talk to regularly.

In two paragraphs: This book is for business owners and top executives who would like to systematically and predictably add organic sales growth. It lays out publicly, for the first time, my simple proactive sales system that more than 400 business-to-business clients have run over the past 20 years. These clients add 20 to 30% sales growth to their top lines year after year. How will you accomplish this? By adding process, accountability, tracking, and scorecards to your sales function to help your people be proactive instead of reactive.

The Outgrow system will drive proactive communications with customers and prospects, and arm you with powerful data and insight about leading indicators of sales success. Your people will systematize following up, constantly expand orders, regularly ask for the business, and consistently talk to the many customers and prospects who don't regularly hear from them. And you will see the analytics in black and white. It works so well because it's so rare: your competition is almost certainly not doing these things. You will find revenue rising predictably, constantly, and in a measurable way, creating growth that you can plan around—because this growth will be created by the repeatable behaviors of your customer-facing people.

Chapter 1

THE OVERVIEW

The Outgrow Selling System for Predictable Revenue Growth

THE REVENUE PROBLEM

Proactive Selling: *Communicating with customers and prospects when they aren't expecting you (unscheduled), and when nothing is wrong.*

The CEO and I sat down at a small conference table in his office for a brief conversation before our meeting with his business unit presidents was set to begin. This was a large company in the wholesale distribution industry, owned by private equity, with the experienced CEO hired within the last year. I wanted to get his assessment of his company's situation before our larger meeting with him and his team.

"Alex," he said, "I have a revenue problem."

Nobody had ever said this to me before, in those words, and I've been talking with company leaders about growing sales for about 20 years.

"Tell me more," I prompted.

"My salespeople are good order takers," he explained. "They're problem solvers. But they're not really salespeople."

We had talked on the phone several times before this in-person meeting, so I went back to my notes.

"But you said you've had solid growth over the last few years?"

He didn't hesitate: "Sure, but prices in our industry have gone way up. It's inflationary growth. We've also acquired some companies. But we've had little to no real organic volume growth created by our salespeople."

And there, in the first three minutes of a three-hour meeting, this CEO defined the issue for nearly all business-to-business companies that rely on a sales team: *salespeople are good at reacting to incoming customer inquiries, issues, problems, and requests, but not so much at proactively creating new and additional business with them.*

How many are this way?

Out of the thousands of business-to-business companies I've talked with in depth over the years, and the hundreds that I've worked closely with, I'm comfortable putting the percentage at 90%. That is, 90% of all companies—*and salespeople*—are basically totally reactive in their interactions with customers.

This has huge implications for so many areas of your business, but I think the biggest one is this: customers experience almost no proactive communications from their suppliers or service providers. Customers call their salespeople usually only when there is a problem and, similarly, salespeople only call customers when . . . there is a problem. In fact, the first thing customers think when one of their salespeople calls is, *What's wrong?* As a result, it's so incredibly easy to stand out from *all* of your competition in this environment.

By being proactive, it's easy to show your customer you care more than your competition does. It's easy to show up, be present, and follow up. It's easy to build better relationships, based on mutual trust, by showing up when nothing is wrong. It won't be long until your customers start telling you, "Nobody follows up with me like you do."

But why are most companies *not* doing this?

Why have so many companies mastered reactive work, but struggle to implement proactive selling? The rest of this chapter will examine the reasons.

WHY MOST SALES ORGANIZATIONS ARE TOTALLY REACTIVE

The reactive approach to business is the default approach. Proactivity requires focus, attention, and intention. Unfortunately, most of us are too busy fighting the proverbial fires of the day brought to us by customers, suppliers, coworkers, and sometimes the economy to even *think* about proactivity. Most people in sales, management, and even executive leadership roles are simply trying not to drown.

Here are 10 reasons I see and hear frequently among my clients that keep organizations from predictably generating proactive revenue growth.

1. **Most inbound and outbound communications with customers require both parties to *react*.** Customers call salespeople with problems: *Where is the product? Why didn't you do what you said? It's too expensive. Even though I'm just telling you about it now, I need you to do this right now!* Also, salespeople tend to only call customers when there is a problem: *I don't have it. I can't get it. The price is going up.*

2. **Culturally, most companies do not focus on organic sales.** It's not in most firms' DNA to communicate proactively. They have never really done so successfully. And they don't really know *how* to.

3. **Owners and CEOs tend to prioritize other initiatives.** Sometimes it feels like top leaders focus on everything *but*

organic growth: hiring people, acquiring companies, buying land, buying or leasing buildings, buying equipment, obtaining safety certifications, rolling out software systems, upgrading technology. All of these things are important leadership pursuits, but none impact the business as much as proactively driving sales. In fact, sales growth drives all of these other initiatives.

4. **Most companies don't invest in their salespeople.** This is interesting because it's the sales function that makes it possible for every other corporate function and job role to even exist. But at many companies, the sales staff usually gets the least amount of training, development, and investment.

5. **There is no customer relationship management (CRM) software.** It's amazing how large a company can grow without technology in place to support its sales function. About half of my clients over $100M in revenue simply do not have a CRM.

6. **There is a CRM, but getting salespeople to use it consistently is an unbearably difficult effort.** Many of the companies that have a CRM often don't use it consistently or correctly. Some of the most popular CRMs are complex and require too much time for salespeople to learn and utilize properly. I have found many salespeople will give a new CRM a brief but honest effort, and what they discover is that extracting useful information is challenging at best. So it doesn't take long before a CRM becomes an elaborate address book filled with names and numbers and little else. It's no wonder salespeople move away from using them.

7. **Most salespeople have a huge fear of rejection.** We will dive deeply into this topic in chapters 2 and 3, but we humans are driven by our fears of failure and rejection. And nobody gets rejected more than salespeople. Nobody experiences more

failure. So when you ask them to go to customers proactively—when they don't absolutely "have to," and when rejection is highly likely—they're not exactly eager to run into that burning building. The psychology isn't on our side.

8. **Most sales growth initiatives focus on mechanics instead of mindset.** Our behavior follows our thinking, and it's impossible for salespeople to outsell their mindset. Basically, the vast majority of growth initiatives do not address the fear that keeps salespeople from proactively selling to begin with. This is why most attempts at "let's call three customers every day from now on" fizzle out and fade away quickly. The fear is much bigger than your request. They *want* to come along with your initiative and help the company grow, but their fear is too big. It's the mindset that keeps people from taking action. So we will focus there. More on this in chapter 2.

9. **Most previous attempts at organic growth have failed.** Most experienced salespeople have been through multiple failed growth initiatives in their career. They have seen these efforts come and go like flavors of the month handed down by the owner or CEO. They expect the same from any new attempt at organic growth. When you tell them, *This time it's different*, they think, *Sure it is!* And then they sit back, watch, and wait it out. And usually, it goes away. Most change does, and things revert to the default—reactive—position.

10. **Most salespeople aren't used to accountability, and most leaders don't know how to implement it with salespeople.** Accountability is difficult to implement in any department of your company. It's most difficult with salespeople, who are independent, entrepreneurial, stubborn, and often not even under your roof because they're on the road. Their attitude is often some version of, *Do you want me to sell, or do you want me*

to spend time logging my calls? And it's hard to give them a good answer to this resistance. I will arm you with several replies to this (valid) concern in chapter 9.

INTRODUCING THE OUTGROW SELLING SYSTEM

Enter the Outgrow Selling System. Used by hundreds of business-to-business sales organizations—including manufacturers, wholesale distributors, and services companies like engineering and consulting firms—this system addresses each of the issues and roadblocks described in the previous section. Here is a detailed overview of the Outgrow Selling System, which is also designed as a preview of the chapters ahead.

Outgrow Is a Culture, Not a Project (Chapter 2)

Projects start and stop, but culture is a permanent reflection of what's important to you as a business owner or top executive. Projects tend to lose energy and focus, often fizzling out before their true impact can be experienced. Culture is known and communicated by all levels of your organization. It's also felt and experienced by your customers.

So what is the Outgrow culture?

- At its core, it's about knowing your great value to your customers and prospects, and behaving accordingly. This means being confident and bold (see next item), but not arrogant. It means showing up, following up, and being present, even when nothing is wrong.

- It makes clear that your people are helping your customers, not selling to them. This has the advantage of being totally true, and it makes it much easier for your salespeople to proactively communicate with customers and prospects.

- Outgrow is led by the top executive of the organization. It is not run by this person, but it is energized and encouraged by them.

- Outgrow is scalable. The largest company to run Outgrow has several billion dollars in annual revenue. I've personally led many companies that earn several million dollars in annual revenue, as well as countless companies in the tens of millions in sales, and also many under $10 million. The smallest companies to run Outgrow are trying to grow to $1 million in sales.

- The system revolves around regular internal communications led by managers. Team by team and location by location, managers will continuously focus on the importance of proactively helping customers. We do this because people only do what they think is important to their boss, and this is how we show them it's important.

- Outgrow asks that salespeople not only do the work, but also quickly show the work by logging it. Because if it's not recorded, did it really happen? And how can it be followed up on if it doesn't exist anywhere? In turn, leaders will be armed with powerful analytics and success stories, which will be shared with the team.

A Mindset Shift Toward Confidence and Boldness Is at the Center of Outgrow (Chapter 2)

Human behavior is generally driven by fear and doing what we can to avoid it. The sales professional is totally motivated by fear, because nobody gets rejected more than those of us who sell. And it is the act of selling that leads to these failures. So we avoid it! (Helpful to the work, right?) This is why so few salespeople are able to be proactive—going to customers puts them in a position for likely rejection and failure.

With the Outgrow system, we help salespeople understand their great value to customers. We show them how much their customers appreciate and need their help. We do this in the customers' own words, letting salespeople hear the people they deal with every day talking about the immense impact of their work.

In turn, salespeople begin to realize the enormous impact they have on their customers, far beyond the products and services being sold. Outgrow salespeople move from fear to confidence, from pessimism to optimism, from cynicism to gratitude, from quick surrenders to perseverance, from focusing on products and services to focusing on their value and the tremendous relationships they build. And when these thinking shifts occur, they lead to the single most important shift: from selling reactively and taking orders to communicating proactively and developing new, organic business.

All Customer-Facing Staff Can Participate in Outgrow (Chapter 3)

Outgrow is a simple process for all of your customer-facing teams: outside salespeople, inside salespeople, customer service people, counter staff if you have them. Some of my clients include delivery drivers if they have a logistics operation, because who sees customers more than them? You will also want to plug in all the managers of these teams, including location or branch managers, as well as executive leaders like vice presidents, presidents, and general managers.

The reason we want to be as inclusive as possible is because Outgrow is based on proactive, outbound communications efforts. And the more people making efforts—or taking swings, as we say—the more successes, or hits, you will experience. With time, and given the advantage of Outgrow data and analytics, you might choose to exclude some nonparticipants. But we start with the maximum, and try to stay there, with the knowledge that we can adjust as needed.

We Focus on the Customers Your Teams Don't Interact with Regularly (Chapter 4)

Most sales teams spend the great majority of their time talking with approximately 20% of their customers. These are the people who frequently call their sales contacts—often with problems, stresses, or issues that need to be resolved. They are the squeaky wheels, but also they are present, active, and you have good relationships with them. One of my clients, the president of a large regional wholesale distributor, calls these customers pawpaws. They are your buddies, your friends.

The other 80% of your customers are some mix of the following:

- Customers who are on autopilot, buying some products and services from you and many others from your competition.

- Customers who buy without talking to you at all (they email or use your e-commerce tools).

- Customers who are buying in decreasing amounts, moving more and more business elsewhere, probably without anyone even really noticing.

- Customers who used to buy from you but stopped altogether.

What do these customer sets have in common? We don't talk to them much. We don't interact much.

They also happen to be your company's lowest-hanging fruit for sales growth. Buyers who are house accounts, even if unintentionally.

Which is why, with Outgrow, we make a concerted effort to speak to these somewhat neglected 80%. You've done the work to earn—and, in most cases, keep—their business. Now let's go do the straightforward work to grow your sales with them.

Outgrow Expands Your Wallet Share with Customers (Chapter 5)

Most customers have you niched. They buy some of what they need from you, and some other products and services from your competition. Even if you can provide these other items, they don't think of you for them. Similarly, and painfully, your salespeople don't think to suggest or offer these products. "If they need it, they'll ask me," salespeople say. This simply cannot happen, because it does not occur to your customers to ask you for it. So Outgrow ensures you suggest additional products and services systematically.

Also, if you have multiple product and service categories or groupings or teams (or silos), we actively cross-sell between them. The Outgrow Selling System emphasizes learning about what other categories of offerings your customers buy and helping them bring that business over to you.

The irony is that most people don't want multiple providers. Most people would rather have "their person" who can supply everything they need, which they can manage with a single relationship. It saves them time. It makes life easier for them. Outgrow helps you become your customers' person, so you can sell them everything they buy from companies like yours.

Outgrow Is Based on Making Fast, Simple, Proactive Communications Requiring Just Minutes per Day (Chapter 6)

Running Outgrow requires just a few minutes per day from leaders, managers, and your customer-facing people. This is one of most valued parts of the system: Outgrow does not demand hours per day, because your people are too busy. Even if we needed an hour a day, it would be too long, and people would avoid executing it.

- A did you know (DYK) question (Did you know we also have product or service X or Y?) takes three seconds to ask.

- A reverse did you know (rDYK) question (What else do you need quoted?) is also a three-second effort.

- Pivoting (Pivot) to the sale (When would you like this delivered? How would you like to pay?) also takes three seconds.

- Following up on a quote takes three seconds.

- Asking for a referral takes three seconds.

- There are a variety of phone calls that take between two minutes (if you're leaving a voicemail) and five minutes (if the person picks up).

The key with all of these actions is repetition, over time. One effort is fine, but won't really grow your sales significantly. What we want is the entire team taking action consistently, for a long time.

Outgrow Tracks and Rewards Swings, Not Hits

Outgrow encourages, tracks, and incentivizes efforts, not successes—swings, not hits. The two major reasons for this are:

1. We can control our behaviors (the efforts or swings) but not whether we get a sale (hits)—that part isn't up to us; it's up to the customer. Focusing on efforts serves the dual purpose of taking pressure off your Outgrowers and making this process totally predictable. As long as your staff is implementing Outgrow actions, your revenue *will* grow.

2. We know what the batting averages are. After tens of millions of actions logged by more than 400 Outgrow companies over about 20 years, I have an accurate idea of the success rates of each Outgrow technique. Consider the following success rates:

Outgrow Success Rates

- **The Voicemail + Text Message (VM+Txt):** 66% return communication

- **The Did You Know Question (DYK):** 20% add line item

- **The Reverse Did You Know Question (rDYK):** 80% name additional products

- **The Pivot to the Sale (Pivot):** 25% say yes

- **Pivot to the Next Conversation (Pivot-C):** 75% schedule the next interaction

- **Percent of Business Question (%Biz):** 40% add on additional product

- **The Internal Referral Request (iRef):** 66% provide internal referral

- **The External Referral Request (xRef):** 66% provide external referral

These success rates and actions are detailed in depth, with multiple scripted examples, in chapter 6.

Outgrow Arms You with a Detailed Weekly Cadence of Play-Calling, Implementing, and Tracking (Chapter 7)

Here is the weekly rhythm of Outgrow: Basically, you assign a target quantity of proactive communications for the week, and your customer-facing people will go and do them. Their efforts will yield powerful data, which can be shared with the group at the end of the week. You can also share their top wins of the week with this work. In more detail:

1. At the start of the week, you will assign a specific quantity of certain communications for your team to make. You might request five proactive calls to customers they haven't talked to in six months or more. And on those calls, they should ask five did you know questions. You can also ask for five quote follow-ups. You might aim them toward certain customers to communicate with.

2. Next, throughout the week, your customer-facing teams will go to their customers and prospects and deliver the communications you have asked to target. Hopefully all of them will do so, but this is probably unlikely. Some of them will, and some of those people will generate much of your growth.

3. As they make their communications in a few minutes a day, your Outgrowers will log their communications into a system. This

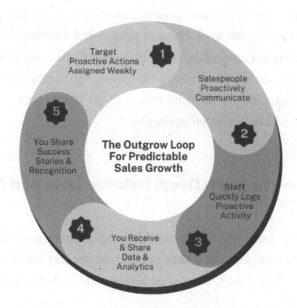

can be inside your CRM—and Outgrow has been implemented in many major CRMs on the market—or, if you don't have a CRM, a simple web form can be designed to capture the opportunities uncovered, as well as the number and types of actions delivered. Outgrowers are also asked to record the estimated (and annualized) value of the opportunity they progressed, quoted, or closed. I'll review the tech options for tracking and sharing these records in chapter 7.

4. From these logs, you get detailed and powerful data outputs. Combined, this data shines a light on leading indicators of your sales health. More communications always lead to more sales, while fewer communications lead to fewer sales. Depending on the length of your sales cycle, there may or may not be a delay between total monthly actions climbing, for example, and your sales following upward. These scorecards can be shared with the group at the end of the week. More on this in the next section, as well as chapter 7.

5. The final part of your Outgrow week is to share the top wins your Outgrowers have generated with the entire sales group. Wins can be business opened, progressed forward, or closed. A consistent recognition program will not only motivate people to give you more Outgrow participation, but also teach everyone in the organization the right things to do. Examples of real client wins will be reviewed in chapter 7.

You'll Be Armed with Deep, Detailed Data and Analytics (Chapter 7)

Outgrow will arm you and your leadership team with layered and detailed data and analytics that accurately predict the future health of your sales function. Outgrow generates additional sales predictably because it's based on behaviors you can control. And we are asking your team to log their behaviors—as driven and requested by you—so that you can see accurate counts of proactive communications. This information will arm you with a variety of analytics. The two most important ones are:

- The leading indicators of sales growth. The sale is the final indicator. But in Outgrow we count all the steps that lead up to the sale: the proactive call, uncovering an opportunity by educating customers on what else you can do for them, following up on these opportunities, and, finally, closing the business. These metrics will tell you what sales will do in the future!

- The metrics tell us which of your salespeople care, and which do not. Because we are only counting efforts (swings) rather than successful sales (hits), you will see who is swinging the bat and who is not. We don't need hits. We only need swings—from as many people as possible, for as long as possible. We're really just measuring who is trying.

You Will Meet with, Guide, and Coach Your Managers and Outgrowers Regularly (Chapter 8)

At its core, Outgrow runs on a weekly cadence as described earlier in this section. To keep this cadence running, a series of strategic and tactical meetings is required. These include Quarterly Planning sessions and one-on-one Monthly Reviews led by leaders with their customer-facing people. But the foundational connection with your team is your Monday Outgrow Huddle (MOH).

The MOH is designed to run for less than 20 minutes, which is why I don't even like to call it a meeting. Its main purpose is to discuss who to reach out to proactively that week. This is where you will review lists of customers (discussed in chapter 4) and help your participants fill out their personal Outgrow Call Planner.

Another important meeting is the one-on-one Monthly Review between a manager and each of their customer-facing people. Here, managers will go over how many proactive communications each of their people made that month, how many opportunities they uncovered, and how much estimated and annual business was opened, proposed or quoted, and closed. They'll discuss the participants' engagement level, any resistance their salespeople may be feeling toward their Outgrow work, and, critically, help them understand the mechanics of the swings and technology tools being used.

You Will Be Armed with Multiple Approaches to Overcoming Resistance and Pushback from Salespeople (Chapter 9)

Because Outgrowers are humans, they struggle with fears and discomforts. These particular humans are also very busy jumping through hoops your customers put up for them. They spend countless hours doing reactive customer service work. As such, some of your people will predictably push back on your Outgrow initiative. After 20 years of implementing this work, I believe I have seen every possible resistance. We will go over an inclusive list in chapter 9, as well as what to do about them to manage staff resistance. For now, here are the three major ones:

- People don't love change. Some hate it. Some of your people have been working the same way for years, maybe decades. Change is uncomfortable.

- Some of your staff will push back hard on the accountability around you setting, expecting, and looking for target sales growth actions. This is one of the centerpieces of this work.

- Some people will fight against the logging and tracking component of this work.

There are myriad ways to deal with these particular forms of resistance, both preemptively (before they occur) and prescriptively (after). We will review them all in chapter 9.

WHAT SEPARATES OUTGROW FROM OTHER SALES SYSTEMS

Outgrow is simple, not complicated.

It's fast—requiring minutes per day, not hours.

It does not require asking people to learn a new model of selling, such as challenging them to implement a technical approach to consultative selling.

Outgrow never tells your salespeople they're doing it wrong. I will never ask you to tear down your current approach and start from scratch. Rather, Outgrow is designed to be superimposed on to your current model of going to the market.

Indeed, Outgrow is a system that emphasizes all that your salespeople do right. It focuses on their incredible value to customers. It helps your salespeople understand this dynamic.

Outgrow is totally scalable. I hear this again and again from Outgrow organizations. It doesn't matter if you are a one-person company or a 3,000-person organization spread across multiple locations around the world. In a few minutes a day, your leaders can choreograph proactive revenue growth across all of your divisions, teams, and locations.

Outgrow is a comprehensive but simple tool kit for your customer-facing staff. It helps them perform better and generate better results—for themselves and for you, their leader. It helps your people serve their customers better and, in turn, it helps your people make more money. As a result, Outgrow will help you retain your staff members.

But Outgrow doesn't only help retain staff. The systematic proactivity leads to strong customer retention—indeed, expansion—because they are hearing from your company, not the competition. This is how you will outgrow your competition.

Outgrow does not ask your people to cold-call, unless it's requisite to their current job role. There is no need for new cold calls here. Rather, we ask individuals to call people they already know. This is comforting and calming. It's nice to talk to friends who are customers. It feels good to help them. This is better than probing and enlarging problems for strangers so that you can solve them, as some selling systems are actually built to do. I believe people have enough actual problems and don't need their salespeople to build problems for them.

Outgrow is an easy system of intentional relationship building so that your salespeople can help more people.

And that's a pretty enjoyable and gratifying way to work—for the customers and absolutely for the salespeople too.

Outgrow is feel-good, relationship-based selling.

OUTGROW CASE STUDY: IT'S A CULTURE, NOT A PROJECT

Throughout the book, I've included detailed case studies. All of the companies featured are my clients who run the Outgrow system for predictable, organic revenue growth. Some of the clients have given me permission to use their names. Others asked me to tell their story anonymously because there is sensitive financial information included. Several stated they don't want their competition to know how or why they've outgrown peers in their industry so significantly. Understandably, they wish to keep Outgrow to themselves. J&B Supply is a third-generation plumbing and HVAC distributor in Arkansas. Before J&B started running Outgrow, the owners, Steve and Brent Jones—father and son—told me company sales had been flat for 13 years. Then they implemented Outgrow, and the company experienced seven consecutive months of double digit–percentage growth.

Here is what average daily sales did, before and after Outgrow:

Average Daily Sales by Quarter

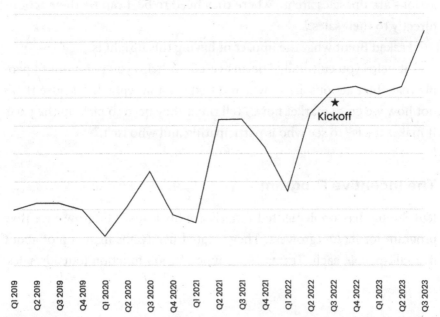

A Culture, Not a Project

Like most Outgrow organizations, J&B thinks of this work as a permanent part of their company, but it didn't necessarily start out that way: "At first we thought of Outgrow as a project, but once we got it going, we decided to make it a culture," said Brent Jones. "We have been consistent with it now for the 18 months we've been running it. Projects have an expiration date. Culture sticks."

The mindset has changed dramatically. "Now they know they are not bugging the customer. They are legitimately helping the customer by asking the extra questions," said Brent. "It's just assumed that they will always ask, 'What else do you need for that project?'"

The Outgrow Analytics

Steve and Brent have been tracking actions since the first day of Outgrow. "I've got averages on every single action," Brent said. "So I know if we need to do more quote follow-ups or post-delivery calls. *I know when actions dip, sales will dip.* When actions are down, sales are down. When actions are up, sales are up where they need to be. I can tie their actions directly to their sales."

I asked Brent what the impact of having this insight is.

"It helps you culturally," he answered. "It helps you point out to people that their actions are down, and that's not acceptable because that's not how we go to market now. I tell them they need to pick up the pace. It makes it easy to see who is participating and who isn't."

The Incentive Program

J&B Supply has implemented a fairly sophisticated Outgrow incentive program for its Outgrowers. They created five teams made up of about five salespeople each. Teams are grouped by job function (outside sales,

Bonus Program

	Springdale	Sherwood	Team Mandaloria	Top Gun	Soonerbacks	Golden Girls	Cobra Kai	Nucleus	Total Actions
7/3/2023	89	2	26	28	51	25	50	52	323
7/10/2023	36	5	-	44	84	64	168	67	468
7/17/2023	20	10	-	40	72	-	280	31	433
7/24/2023	34	7	-	46	56	60	106	33	342
7/31/2023	60	12	-	46	64	50	72	75	379
8/7/2023	32	21	-	44	94	102	137	35	465
8/14/2023	-	4	-	44	85	85	141	-	359
8/21/2023	27	22	-	40	62	27	162	46	386
8/28/2023	25	56	-	37	88	-	78	-	282
9/4/2023									
9/11/2023									
9/18/2023									
9/25/2023									
Total Q3 Actions	323	139	26	369	656	413	1,172	339	
Total Projected	467	201	38	533	948	597	1,693	490	
Goal Tier 1	208	208	104	208	520	312	520	256	
Goal Tier 2	390	390	195	390	975	585	975	480	

inside sales, showroom sales, etc.). It's a quarterly bonus program, based strictly on Outgrow actions, not sales or line items.

The payout is based on actions, per person, per week, for the whole team. If the team averages eight actions per person, per week, for the quarter, the entire team attains the first tier of the bonus. If the team averages 15 actions per person, per week, they attain the second tier of the bonus. Everybody gets paid the same amount—those with the most actions, and those with the least actions. As you might imagine, this creates some healthy competition between teams, and also some peer pressure within teams. Nobody wants to be the reason that the entire team doesn't get paid.

Outgrow Helps to Hire Salespeople

J&B Supply has also shifted its view of the type of salespeople it seeks to recruit. Experience and product knowledge matter less. Enthusiasm and positivity (which are the only traits that are not teachable) matter more. "Outgrow helps us pinpoint the type of salesperson we're going after," Brent said. "Yes, product knowledge matters, but now we look for somebody willing to learn Outgrow and talk to our customers proactively. You want somebody who will buy into your system. You want somebody with enthusiasm and energy."

Sharing Success Stories

With each week's scorecard, Brent sends the team success stories from the week. Here's what that looks like.

This kind of recognition has immense benefits inside the company:

- It makes the salespeople being featured proud and excited.

- It teaches the Outgrow principles to all participants.

- It makes those not being recognized aspire to be recognized next.

- It maximizes energy and enthusiasm for Outgrow.

From Zero to a Lot

Consider this customer story from Steve, which he calls a *home run story*: "I'll never forget the day we did our kickoff workshop and you sent our folks out of the room to make an initial proactive call to a customer. One of our showroom salespeople, Carol, made a contact with a customer that day. He had been a customer for a long, long time, but hadn't bought anything in years. *We fell off his radar.*

"Last month alone, his statement with us was for $79,000. I know there has been at least $250,000 in business with this guy since. And all she did was let him know we missed his business, and we care about him."

There have been many customers like this at J&B Supply.

There are customers like this at *your* company.

SUCCESS STORIES

"Haven't heard from christian in a couple of weeks. Called him to see if he needed a delivery to the shop and he gave me an order for $2,146."

"I called Aaron on Tuesday to see if he needed anything pulled for the day. He gave me two orders that he needed delivered. Both orders together came out to $2,981."

"I called Nathan --- because I hadn't heard from him in a while. I asked if there was anything I could do for him. He gave me the opportunity to quote a 4 ton system. He called me back about 30 minutes later and gave me the order and added several more items. $4,194.21."

"I called David --- to follow up on a quote I did for him last week to see if he had heard anything. I let him know that we had everything in stock. He told me that he would call me back after he called his customer. About 30 minutes later, he called me back to give me a PO and address for delivery. Order totaling $3,412.00."

"I reached out to Chuck at Ca---t after we delivered a large order to them. Everything was great. I asked about a quote that I have out to them for another larger order. We discussed the grant money that was still available. He told me that they just got the go ahead to get it ordered and he gave me a PO# for $19,075. Nice order!!"

"The phone call I made to a customer that hasn't done business with us for a while during our first meeting with Alex has turned into a total of $59,400.00 so far. I called to see if they needed anything else and added $1,260.00 this morning."

Chapter 2

THE CULTURE
AND MINDSET

A bout 60% of launching Outgrow in your firm is mindset work, which is what this chapter focuses on. Because behavior follows mindset—and because it's impossible for a salesperson, *and an organization*, to outsell its mindset—shifting to a confident, optimistic, persevering, and proactive mindset is one of the most important parts of this work.

This chapter deals with what the Outgrow culture is, and the all-important mindset shifts that turn a reactive sales organization into a proactive one. We will also dive deeply into *how* to create these shifts.

What Outgrow Companies Believe	How Outgrow Companies Behave
You are helping, not selling.	Outgrow is led by the CEO/owner and supported strongly by leadership.
Customers want and *need* to hear from you.	Team managers are the key to your Outgrow success.
It would hurt customers to not be proactive.	Salespeople must regularly hear about their great value to customers.
Customers are buying elsewhere what they should be buying from you.	Outgrow is a part of the daily conversation at your organization.
The rest of your company *relies* on this proactive business development work.	Outgrow is logged and tracked.
Outgrow makes you stand out from the competition.	Outgrowers show up, follow up, and seek to help their customers more.

No weeks off . . .
The Outgrow gas pedal stays pushed!

WHAT OUTGROW COMPANIES BELIEVE

My clients often tell me that Outgrow is a culture, not a project.

What's the difference? Projects start and stop, but your company culture is a lot more permanent. Projects go away with time, but culture remains over time—even as employees come and go. Specifically, I believe culture is made of: (1) what the people inside your company believe, and (2) how they behave. So, let's dive into both components.

You Are Helping, Not Selling

Companies running Outgrow understand their tremendous value to customers, and as a result, they believe they are *helping*, not selling, when they communicate proactively. Everybody wants to be helped. In millions of proactive communications logged and tracked by more than 400 clients, I've never once heard of a customer saying, "Thanks, but I'd rather not be helped today." And I've never heard of a customer saying, "I don't want you to make my life easier today."

Outgrow firms believe customers are better off doing business with you than with the competition. They are totally confident that they save their customers more time, deliver faster, are more available, are more creative, think farther outside the box, and have better friendships with customers than the competition does. This is a pretty good way to do business!

Customers Want—and Need—to Hear from You

As a result of how well you help customers, Outgrow firms believe that not only do customers want to hear from your salespeople, but they *need* to hear from them. Because when your people show up, they make customers' lives easier. They help customers with upcoming needs, without the customer having to ask for it or even *think* of it. Your salespeople will show up and say, "I was thinking about you. It's important to me to help you." Customers value this because it's incredibly rare and, yes, helpful. They appreciate it because you are saving them from having to think about it again.

It Would Be a Disservice to Your Customers to Not Do This Work

Conversely, Outgrow companies believe that if they *don't* show up proactively, they are not only choosing not to help their valued customers, but they are choosing to hurt them. How are your customers hurt when you are not proactive? They have to deal with your competition, which is not nearly as good as you are. They have to wait longer, experience delays in delivery, and work with somebody who doesn't treat them as well as you do. You are also forcing them to have to take additional time from their day to ask others for products and services that you could have helped them with proactively. They don't deserve this from you.

Customers Are Buying Products and Services Elsewhere That They Should Be Buying from You

Right now, as you read this, many of your customers are buying things from the competition that they could be buying from you. How many? Depending on the business, the answer is somewhere between *most* and *many*. This is at once terribly painful and a gigantic opportunity. Painful because you would like to sell them these additional products and services, and they would like to buy them from you instead of from providers who aren't as good as you. This doesn't happen today, in most cases, because your salespeople simply haven't proactively communicated enough. And, of course, it's a huge opportunity because it's such low-hanging fruit—and so much of it! Outgrow companies believe in harvesting this fruit.

The Rest of the Company Relies on Outgrowers

Companies running Outgrow believe that everyone at the firm who doesn't sell—the service providers, the delivery drivers, the warehouse workers, the back-office people, the technical people—rely on Outgrowers showing up, following up, and being proactive. Salespeople are lucky because they get to directly impact the size and success of your company. But everyone else who helps deliver what is sold—and those who do the work to keep a business operating—don't get to exert nearly the same influence. Those people deserve to work in a thriving, fast-growing organization. And Outgrowers can literally make it so.

Outgrow Makes You Stand Out from the Competition

Outgrow companies know that their competition isn't doing this communication work. They understand that customers only hear from suppliers when there is a problem or stressful situation. This gives Outgrow firms and their salespeople a gigantic competitive advantage, because we show up when nothing is wrong. We show up to check in on customers, ask about their families, and ask what else they have coming up that we can help them with. We follow up, but others do not. We systematically suggest additional products or services, but most others do not.

Internet marketing and social media have leveled the playing field to where websites, voices, and approaches are all relatively similar. A Google search listing or ad, a Facebook ad, or a LinkedIn post generally don't do much to help you stand out from the crowd. But Outgrow Proactive Communications (OPCs) sure do. They make you singular because customers always remember who has been actively trying to help them and who has been silent. And even if they don't have a need at the moment your salespeople are calling, where do you think they will go when the need does arise? They will go to the providers who have been showing up, following up, and trying to help. They will go to companies running Outgrow.

HOW OUTGROW COMPANIES BEHAVE

Now that we've covered the beliefs that Outgrow companies share, let's look at the key behaviors and actions that lead to successfully implementing predictable organic revenue growth.

Outgrow Is Led by the Owner or CEO

Outgrow is an initiative that must be fronted by the top executive in the business, typically the owners or the CEO. Outgrow is usually a foundational change for the organizations implementing it—that is, they're not systematically proactive now, but they're trying to become so. It's change that involves shifting mindsets around what is often uncomfortable behavior, as well as incorporating accountability, tracking, metrics, and even incentives. You can see how this change cannot be successfully made from the middle of an organization. It requires the owner or chief executive.

It's important to note here that the top executive does not need to run the initiative. You do not need to do the administrative work of running the process. This means that unless you are a very small business, you probably don't need to set the target actions, create the logging mechanisms, manipulate the scorecards, and report to your group about the success.

So what *is* your role? It is to visibly lead the charge on Outgrow. To lend it energy and enthusiasm. To make it clear to your team that it is important to you. People only do what they feel is important to their leaders. More on all this in the next chapter.

It Is Strongly Supported by the Top Leadership Team

Your direct reports should also display full and obvious support of Outgrow. There must be no doubts among your frontline people that the company's leadership believes in—and expects—proactive organic revenue growth. If people have doubts, they probably won't do the quick, straightforward, but uncomfortable work that Outgrow entails. Why would leadership *not* support the Outgrow program? Here are some reasons I have seen among my clients:

- Accountability is uncomfortable, especially for leaders who have not held people accountable in the past—which is, unfortunately, most leaders.

- It's change. It's new. And humans tend not to like that.

- Also, change tends to go away and not stick. All of your people, even the senior leaders, expect your new initiatives to fade away. Most people have career experience watching new programs come and go. They are assuming that Outgrow is just another "flavor of the month." With time and consistency, you will prove them wrong.

- Because they are senior leaders, they are probably operating with a depth of experience in your industry. Very experienced leaders often feel they know how to do things because "I've been doing this a long time." For some, this kind of structure can almost seem like an affront, because they think, *Believe me, I know what I'm doing.*

I'll dig in to dealing with challenges, obstacles, and overcoming resistance in chapter 9.

Managers Are the Key to Your Outgrow Success

Many of my clients have multiple teams, often at multiple locations. These groups all report to a manager, whose job title can include:

- Inside or Outside Sales Manager

- Branch or Location Manager

- Client Executive for Service Companies

- Team Leader

- Project Manager

For our purposes, a manager is somebody who has frontline customer-facing people reporting to them. We will go over their role in the Outgrow program in detail in the next chapter, but the team goes as the manager goes. If you have five teams, and three managers are bought in but two are not, you will probably find that those two teams are not participating in Outgrow. A manager has exponential impact on your proactive, organic revenue growth, because they lead multiple team members. And because you cannot be with multiple teams in multiple places at once, the mid-level manager is the single most important role in your Outgrow success. Their buy-in is essential, and I will expound at length on how to gain and keep this throughout the rest of the book, particularly in chapters 3, 7, and 9.

Salespeople Must Regularly Hear About Their Immense Value to Customers

One of the more important cultural elements of Outgrow is exposing your customer-facing staff to the warm-and-fuzzy, glowing feedback of your happy customers. This is critical because happy customers do not generally tell you what they love about working with you. It doesn't come in on its own, does it? So we need to go get it. I dive into this process deeply in the next section of this chapter. But I want to plant the seed with you here: we tackle fear and discomfort and build confidence and perseverance by obtaining and sharing testimonials from happy customers.

It's a foundational principle in Outgrow: your salespeople don't know how valuable they are because they deal with problems and stresses that your customers bring them all day long. Despite this, they are hugely valued by your customers. We must show them this in the words and voices of the customers they spend their time helping. If *you*, the top executive, told them they were wonderful, your team would want to know what new work you want them to do. If *I* told them they were great, they would rightfully push back and tell me I'm a consultant, how do I know? Again, they'd be right.

But when the paying customer talks about how excellent they are, it is simply the truth. And it cannot be argued against.

Because it is fact.

Outgrow Is a Part of the Daily Conversation

The companies that talk about Outgrow the most grow the most and the fastest. It is brought up in meetings, even when it is not the central topic. There are Monday Outgrow Huddles (MOH) that set up the week, and Outgrow Monthly Reviews, which are one-on-one conversations between managers and customer-facing reports.

Sometimes, my clients place customer testimonials on their office walls. This way, their staff is literally surrounded by customer positivity and motivation, which grows confidence. Other companies will hang additional products and services to suggest on the walls so that customer-facing people are reminded of what did you know questions to ask about.

Some of my clients place scorecards in easy-to-see places in the office, and still others display "swings leaders" on large wall-mounted monitors. Additionally, staff is encouraged to share proactive selling success stories with each other.

Outgrow Is Logged and Tracked

Outgrow companies make it a point to log their proactive actions and the opportunities that arise from them. Logging actions, or swings, as my clients and I often call them, is important for several reasons:

1. It arms you with powerful leading indicators of sales growth. These are measures of sales success that come prior to the sale.

2. It gives you scorecards and rankings of involvement and participation. This lets you know who is trying because all we're doing is measuring effort, not closed sales; we track proactive communications. And you will also quickly see who is not giving you simple effort. We're asking for five minutes of proactivity a day, which leads to immensely rewarding results. But still, only some of the people will come along with your initiative.

3. Logging proactive communications and their outcomes gives salespeople, managers, company leaders, and all the people who interact with that customer both a log of communications, so everyone is aware of what has transpired, and an incredibly valuable list of opportunities to follow up on. If it is not logged, it does not exist anywhere except in the salesperson's fading memory. And that is not a reliable system on which to base your sales growth.

Outgrowers Show Up, Follow Up, and Seek to Help Their Customers More

I've mentioned this behavior multiple times, but it is the key differentiator between an Outgrow salesperson and others: Outgrowers show up when nothing is wrong. A problem is not required for an Outgrower to reach out to a customer. A proactive conversation is completely different from a reactive problem-solving exchange that makes up 90% of most salespeople's interactions and 90% of your competition's regular experience. A proactive communication strategy invites customers to take a breath and consider what they have upcoming that you may be able to help with. They can consider which additional products and services may be valuable. In that moment, they are not panicked or stressed as it relates to their business with you. This is the exact opposite of a reactive customer service conversation. These conversations are so completely different that they use different parts of the brain. That's why it's impossible for both the customer and the salesperson to think proactively and reactively at the same time.

This is why Outgrowers show up when nothing is wrong: to allow the customer to do additional business with them. We also follow up on opportunities, quotes, and proposals regularly. We are consistent about this. And we always ask different versions of this question: "What else do you have coming up that I can help you with?" This is how we help them think about what else they might need from us.

No Weeks Off; the Gas Stays Pushed

Implementing Outgrow is an exercise in building and maintaining a new habit. Habits require a mindset shift (which I will cover in depth in the next section of this chapter) and, of course, new behaviors. Some people will come around quickly and easily, while others will be more challenging to bring along. Once you have Outgrow implemented and running, it should be permanent and consistent.

There should be no weeks off, even on the weeks that *you*—the top leader—don't feel like pushing for accountability. I've seen it again and again: once leaders let their foot off the gas of a new initiative, it becomes *very* difficult to bring it back. The first time you show your people that it's okay to take a break from Outgrow—or pretty much *any* new initiative—is often enough to make it drift away entirely, and permanently.

On the first "pause," you'll permanently lose a few people and see several people become less committed. Why risk this? It takes focus and significant effort to build a habit of proactivity and get people implementing new behaviors. With corporate change, permanent consistency is everything.

THE OUTGROW MINDSET

Much of my work with clients revolves around the research findings from the field of positive psychology. This entire field is led by Martin Seligman, who is the director of the Center of Positive Psychology at the University of Pennsylvania. I studied his work as a premed psychology major in college, and also in graduate school when I attended a doctoral program in clinical psychology. That's right, I went to school to become a therapist, and I realized very early in the first year, as a 21-year-old, that it was not for me. But even though I left the formal study of clinical psychology, the deep understanding I gained about human thinking and behavior—and specifically positive psychology—has been the foundation of my work as a revenue growth consultant.

What is positive psychology? It's the study of what makes us happy and successful, as opposed to the rest of psychology, which studies human deficiencies and diseases like depression, anxiety, addiction, and much more. Positive psychology focuses on areas like optimism, gratitude, and how grateful professionals outperform and go further in their careers than those who are not grateful.

Martin Seligman has done a lot of the seminal work in this field. In 1991, Seligman wrote a book called *Learned Optimism*, which argues—for one of the very first times—that we can make ourselves more optimistic. In 1995, he followed that up with *The Optimistic Child*, which played an important role in how my wife, Lisa, and I raised our kids. Optimism, he wrote, can immunize children and adults alike against depression.

Another key component in positive psychology is perseverance, the idea that not giving up has a huge influence on human success. This is especially true in the selling profession.

I will dive deeply into the mindsets of confidence, optimism, boldness, and perseverance later in this chapter. For now, let's zoom out and look at the success-determining role that mindset plays in revenue growth.

In Business, a Growth Mindset Is Everything

Behavior follows thinking, always.

As such, it's impossible for the individual salesperson to outsell their thinking, and it's impossible for teams to outperform the mindset that's prevalent in the group.

If salespeople believe they are bothering the customer and seek to avoid rejections (as humans do), they will sell accordingly: timidly, meekly, reactively, waiting for the customer to call them and inquire about products and services. On the other hand, if they believe they are helping the customer in amazing ways—which is exactly what your happy customers will tell them when they ask—they will behave this way: confidently, boldly, and trying to help.

The major reason that most corporate change starts, stops, and usually goes away is that the change initiative does not address mindset—the thinking and psychology of the people being asked to change their workday behaviors in order to make change in the company. Your salespeople want to come along with leadership's plans, but their fear and discomfort are much stronger than your request to follow up and make some proactive calls. It's a simple request, but the fear is like a brick wall blocking proactivity.

But where does this fear come from?

The fear comes from working in a profession that revolves around rejection, stress, and a heavy workload.

This Default Mindset Is a Brick Wall for Sales Growth

Stress and failure. Failure and stress. Welcome to the lives of customer-facing people. This is where the fear of failure, rejection, and bothering the customer comes from: They're scrambling from one issue to the next, nearly every interaction is negative and stressful, and most result in *not* winning the business. This is the default starting position for most salespeople and sales departments. It's also contagious, and quickly spreads to the entire group, especially your newer hires and the less experienced people. You can see how this default thinking is totally antithetical to the work that proactive growth requires, which is being systematically proactive, communicating about products and services that customers are not buying, and reaching out to customers and prospects they don't normally talk to.

Helping customer-facing people overcome this default thinking is the first and most important step in becoming a company with predictable organic growth. If you want to run Outgrow and expand revenue systematically, you'll need salespeople who are more confident and bolder than they are today. If we don't acknowledge and help people past these fears and discomforts, nothing else in Outgrow—the showing up for customers, the following up, the expanding wallet share by adding products and services—can stick over time. These things might start to pick up briefly, but the default fears and discomforts will overwhelm any initial action.

So how exactly do we help people with these fears and discomforts? It's the very first thing that happens in Outgrow.

How to Help Salespeople Get Past Their Fears

Outgrow helps your sales team and other customer-facing people move past their fears and discomforts at the start of the implementation, and then continues focusing on developing a positive, optimistic, and bold mindset. It's a three-part effort:

Step One: Show Your People How Good They Are, in Their Own Customers' Words

We marinate them in the positivity of your company's happy customers. This jars their thinking out of reactive-fearful mode. It shocks them out of their default position of discomfort with showing up and following up.

Of course, this cannot immediately undo years—or a career's worth—of reactivity and fear, but it quickly helps them take a step away from it. The first time we take salespeople through the warm and positive feedback of their happy customers, they are immediately more confident, happy, and optimistic, and nearly instantly more open and receptive to doing the kinds of proactive communications we are asking them to engage in. I dive in to how to do this in the very next section.

Step Two: Constantly Focus on Their Wins, Successes, and Positive Results

We elevate, analyze, and recognize the success proactive efforts have yielded. One of the more important parts of the Outgrow system is to recognize the good work your people have done. We regularly internally communicate the stories of the wins generated by their proactivity, including business opened, progressed forward, or closed. Even if they've been trying to connect with a customer for a long time, and finally scheduled a conversation as a result of an Outgrow communication, that's a win to be shared. It was dormant business, and now there's a sales conversation on the calendar. That's important. Chapter 7 will dive more deeply into the Outgrow Internal Recognition program.

Step Three: Continue Sharing Customer Love Long Term

For years, my clients used their customer recordings and testimonials only at the beginning of their Outgrow implementation. This effectively accomplished Step One: showing your staff how valued, appreciated, and important they are in your customers' lives. This customer love was shared in the Outgrow Launch Workshop—which is the one-day program we use to teach your team the Outgrow work—with staff, but then they returned to reactive, problem-solving, customer service lives. And this everyday stress overwhelms any of the new confidence and positivity and enthusiasm we built in the Outgrow Launch Workshop. That's why it's critical to trickle testimonials to your staff on a regular basis. This continually reminds them of their tremendous impact beyond products and services. This step is critical for long-term buy-in and overcoming resistance to proactivity. It's like a hydration IV: drip by drip, bringing goodness and energy to your salesforce.

One more thing here: customer testimonials and feedback should be refreshed regularly. That is, do a new batch of testimonial interviews (detailed later in this chapter) at least annually, preferably every six months. This way, your people aren't hearing from the same customers over and over again for years.

THE INCREDIBLE POWER OF INTERVIEWING YOUR HAPPY CUSTOMERS

Here are the top 10 immense benefits that interviewing your happy customers about *exactly what they are happy about* will create for your business:

1. You will learn. Your customers will tell you what is working well so you can do more of it.

2. Your people will marinate in positive feedback. This is not

something that happens during the course of their normal days, even though they do tremendously valuable work.

3. The positive feedback will shift your people's mindsets. This is incredibly valuable because it counteracts all the negative and stressful inputs they receive throughout the day from customers.

4. You will hear directly from customers. You are recording the call, with the customers' permission, so your staff will literally hear *their* customers' voices talking about what they love about working with your people.

5. You will pour cement on your relationship with the customers you are talking to because you are asking them for feedback about your work together. They probably don't have any other providers who take the time to do this.

6. Customers will pour cement on their relationship with you by thinking and talking about the wonderful things you do for them.

7. At first, your people will be surprised. "Wow," they will say. "*This is what I do?*" They will be shocked out of their daily work of putting out fires.

8. Next, it will dawn on them: "I'm really helping these customers. I'm not just selling them products or services."

9. Finally, the holy grail: "I guess I'm better than I think!" *Yes!* This is the purpose of interviewing happy customers. Because so many of your salespeople are better than they think they are. And, if behavior follows beliefs, then we need them to know exactly how good their customers think they are so they can behave accordingly.

10. As a result of all of this, your customer-facing people will become more confident, more enthusiastic, more positive, more optimistic, more proactive, and more bold. They will

feel more comfortable with intentional, systematic, proactive communication with customers and prospects, for the express purpose of growing sales.

Basically, the equation goes like this: the more you can expose your customer-facing people to the positive experience of their happy customers, the more revenue they will create for you. Here are some tips for how to interview happy customers to change your people's mindset.

These Are Calls, Not Online Surveys

Completing internet surveys is a chore. It's the only pathway for customer feedback most people ever receive. It takes time, can be a pain, and most people don't appreciate needing to do it. But a proactive, 20-minute call asking for feedback in a conversation is nearly unheard of. It's totally singular. You have a relationship with these folks. They will be happy to talk with you about how to serve them better.

Who Should You Interview?

Go to your happy customers for these conversations. We don't want the complaining or unhappy ones, because they are calling you all day, and your people are talking with them already. Approach the customers who have been with you for some time, and who you know are pleased. The irony is that your salespeople don't talk to them much precisely because there's nothing really wrong. They don't call your people, and your people don't call them.

How Many Customers Should Be Interviewed?

Five conversations will get you 100 minutes of positive, warm-and-fuzzy feedback. Ten customers is a good number. You don't need dozens or more customers. A few go a long way. Also, because most companies are consistent in their service, customers begin to repeat what others have said—so you will find great consistency in the feedback. This is a positive, of course, but it's also why 10 customers in the initial round of interviews is more than enough.

How Should You Set the Call Up?

Email or text your customer to schedule the interview. "We are reaching out to our best customers to get some feedback on how we are doing. Would you please speak with [me, or the salesperson] for 20 minutes? It would help us serve you better."

Who Should Interview Happy Customers?

Your salespeople can do the interviews. Or you can. Or managers can. Or, maybe your Outgrow Advisor. It doesn't really matter who conducts the interview, as long as everyone can listen to it. That means you need to record the call, and ask permission to do so at the top of the conversation.

How Should the Call Go?

You will open the call with a setup:

We'll talk for 20 minutes or so if that still works for you. I'm interested in your thoughts and experience with working with us. Sound okay? Is it okay with you if I record the call, please? (Ninety-nine percent say it's no problem to record—this is because you have a trusting relationship with these folks.)

Then you will work your way through the questions in the next section. Feel free to add your own. You will ask the questions one at a time and then stay quiet until the customer answers. Be comfortable listening and reacting with follow-up questions.

At the end of the call, ask for permission to use their comments.

Thank you so much for this wonderful feedback. I appreciate it so much. Is it okay with you if we use some of your comments in our materials? Note: Ask just like this, broadly, about *materials*. It's broad on purpose and grants use in marketing materials internally, and training materials internally.

Nearly everyone says yes, because they've just finished glowing about you for an extended period of time.

What Questions Should You Ask?

Basically, you are asking them to tell you what they are happy about. That's why every question seeks positive feedback. *Do not ask what you can do better.* You get calls about that all day long. You will want to ask what you can do better. Fight that urge. That's not what these calls are for. Remember the purpose: the commentary you get will be used to marinate your customer-facing people in positivity and love from your company's customers. The reason we are even doing these calls is to increase your people's confidence. Here is what you should ask, in this order:

- *Is it okay with you if I record the call?*

- *What are some of your favorite things about working with us?* The first of the two most important questions on the call.

- *How does that help you?* The second of the two most important questions on the call.

- Listen and follow up with questions like:
    - *Why?*
    - *How?*
    - *In what way?*
    - *Tell me more.*
    - *Why do you say that?*

- Listen actively:
    - *Really?*
    - *That's interesting!*
    - *Wow.*

- How many suppliers/providers/consultants do you work with?
  - *And if you ranked them from best to worst on the kinds of things we're talking about here—like X, Y, Z (repeat some of the items they listed in response to the questions above)—where would you rank us on that list?*
  - *Interesting—is there anything else that puts us there?*

- Tell me about how you view your relationship with our company.
  - *What's it like to work with us?*
  - *How do you feel about that?*
  - *What are the first three descriptive words that come to your mind when you think about working with us?*

How Much Talking Should You Do?

Almost none.

You should ask questions and get out of the way.

Let the customer do 95% of the talking.

When you think they're done answering a question, wait two or three seconds before speaking to make sure. In more than half of these instances, they will start talking again and tell you something you didn't even ask about—and something you would not have even *known* to ask about.

Practice being quiet while the customer thinks. Taking notes helps. Although I've done many thousands of these interviews for clients, and although I record all the calls, I still type notes of nearly every word the customer says. This forces me to stay silent while I type what they say. It's my secret and very basic way to keep my mouth shut while I catch up on my notes.

Frequently, I will say, "Catching up—I'm taking notes while you're talking," and the customer will almost always say, "Oh, no problem, take your time," and then after a short pause, they speak into the silence with even more extremely valuable thoughts and information.

They should be allowed to speak into the silence, but we should stay out of it.

Leave No Room for Negativity

Note that none of the questions ask about what you can do better or what can be improved. These are calls to happy customers, so the questions are intentionally inviting them to talk about what they're pleased with. That's the information we want to bring to the eyes and ears of your sales and customer service people.

If they request to give some constructive feedback, absolutely let them, but then move the conversation back to positivity. I often say, "Thank you for sharing that—I appreciate it. I'll make sure [your salesperson or the owner] sees it. May I ask another question?" And then I maneuver to something they said earlier and continue with the questions.

How to Use These Testimonials

There are two major ways to utilize the positive feedback you gather. I think of them as *confidence shock* and *maintenance*:

1. First, gather your team together and play some of the recordings in their entirety. Pause and discuss key takeaways. Put the major testimonials in writing, and let your people *see* the feedback and *hear* it. Let them marinate in the incredible experiences their customers are discussing. This is the step that shocks them out of their fears and discomforts.

2. Next, put these testimonials in front of your people regularly. Cut 30- to 60-second clips from the audio and play them in meetings. Take three or four testimonials and email them to the group. Put them on the walls. Surround your people in customer positivity to combat the negativity they deal with throughout the day. This is maintenance work. It keeps people confident,

positive, and enthusiastic and in a mindset to do the proactive work we are asking for.

THE MINDSET SHIFTS THAT OCCUR

The following mindset shifts occur fairly quickly for companies that run Outgrow. You should expect these changes in the first 90 days of running Outgrow.

Outgrowers Are Confident Instead of Afraid

When nearly every sales interaction leads to failure or a rejection perceived as personal, salespeople avoid it. Similarly, it makes sense that customer service people—or, more so, highly educated professionals like "seller-doer" engineers, architects, or consultants—avoid proactive selling like the plague. *I'm not going to call when I don't have to and walk into another rejection.*

When Outgrowers hear their customers glowing about them, and talking about what they love about working with them, they rapidly move from fear to confidence. This one mindset shift alone can add 10% organic growth to your top line.

Confident salespeople pick up the phone when nothing is wrong. Fearful salespeople wait for the customer to call them.

Confident salespeople offer additional products and services consistently—almost *religiously*—while fearful salespeople say, "If they need it, they'll call me." Of course, this is impossible because customers don't think of you for products and services they don't already buy.

Confident salespeople follow up on proposals and quotes. Fearful ones wait and wonder: *Don't they want it? Are they mad at me? Why aren't they calling?*

Confident salespeople ask for referrals: "Who else works at your company who I can help the way that I help you?" This is a powerful question because your customers often have multiple buyers, and it's rare that *all of them* are buying from you.

All of this applies to your inside and outside salespeople, and, if you have them, your customer service people, your professional service providers, and even your delivery drivers.

Confident customer-facing people create intentional, organic revenue growth. Fearful ones jump through hoops, on request.

Which would you rather build your company around?

Outgrowers Are Optimistic Instead of Pessimistic

Optimism is one of those mindsets that's rare and separates your team from the competition.

Optimists believe the customer needs their help, and do what they can to provide it. Pessimists believe they are bothering the customer and try to avoid it.

Optimists follow up on proposals and quotes because they believe the customer wants to—*needs to*—do business with them. Pessimists avoid following up because they expect rejection. *Why try? They're just going to say no.*

Ever watch the news on television? Or read it on one of the major online news sites? Is it positive or negative? Optimistic or pessimistic?

Ever read the comments on an online news story? Optimistic or pessimistic?

What about your favorite sports team? Ever read the comments on sports stories? *Sell the team!* they scream. *Fire everyone!* they demand.

One more: Ever check out political surveys? There's often a question on these concerning whether respondents feel the country is moving in the right direction or the wrong direction. Almost always, no matter how good the economy, or how low the unemployment rate, the great majority of people feel that we are moving in the wrong direction.

So it's not just in business or in the sales profession—positive, optimistic people are few and far between and incredibly rare to come across. It's striking when we do, right?

But the *optimistic salesperson* is an even rarer breed.

Maybe 10% qualify, in my experience.

So, if we can get your people to understand their immense value and experience *and expect* success when they communicate proactively, you will enjoy growth that your competition simply cannot create.

Pessimists don't generate predictable organic growth.

Optimists do.

Outgrowers Are Boldly Proactive Instead of Meekly Reactive

Boldness and proactivity are mindsets that present themselves in people's approach to any type of job, but especially sales work. They go together, meaning bold salespeople tend to be proactive, and meek salespeople tend to be reactive. So here are some facts about sales teams that are bold and proactive, instead of meek and reactive:

- **Bold and proactive sales teams take more action.** They procrastinate less. They make communications to customers without overthinking them. They implement a *Ready? FIRE! Aim.* approach to growth because they know we don't need to help the *perfect* customer; we just need to help customers. They know we don't need to offer the *perfect* additional product or service; we just need to suggest things we think will be beneficial to the customers.

- **Bold and proactive sales teams show up for customers when nothing is wrong.** As we've discussed, they don't wait to communicate until something is wrong.

- **Bold and proactive sales teams *take market share from the competition*.** You can't do this reactively. It's a proactive behavior, implemented repeatedly, by as many of your firm's people as possible, for as long as possible. Expanding your wallet share with customers is how to grow, even when your industry may not be. Systematically taking market share elevates you above market conditions. It's a nice way to live. It's how my clients live.

- **Bold and proactive sales teams regularly ask for the business**, because they know every conversation is an opportunity to help their customers, who depend on them for their own work. These salespeople pivot to the sale because they simply assume that the customer needs their help, or else they wouldn't be talking with them. This, of course, has the added benefit of being totally true and correct.

- **Bold and proactive sales teams never worry about bothering the customer** because they understand the tremendous value they bring customers. They understand how rarely a customer hears from a salesperson when there is no problem. They know the customer appreciates hearing from them, because it saves them time. When your salespeople call your customers proactively and ask them what's coming up that they can help with, they are saving the customer from having to think about it again. They can just take care of it now. And that is extremely valuable.

- **Bold and proactive sales teams know that meekness is unfair to customers.** Customers choose you instead of the competition over and over, for years. They deserve more than your team simply taking orders and fixing problems. They deserve to know what else they can buy from you. They deserve the maximum amount of help you can provide. They *do not* deserve having to seek elsewhere the products and services that you can help them with. It's not fair to them. They're good to your company. Outgrowers are good back.

Outgrowers Focus on the Relationship and Value Instead of the Products and Services

Most of us don't sell products or services that are totally singular. That is, our customers have other options. So why do our customers buy products they can get elsewhere from us? Because our version of the product or service is the very best? Almost always, no. They buy it from you not because your products and services are special, but because of the experience of buying it from you.

When I interview customers during the calls detailed earlier in this chapter, here is what they tell me: We [your customers] have been with you for years because it's *easy* to buy from you. It's enjoyable. You do what you say you will (which is, surprisingly, quite rare in business). You are available when we need you, and you are easy to reach. You pick up your phone at night, and on the weekend.

"We've grown up in the business together," they often say.

"We're friends," they say.

And, sometimes, even, "She's like family."

What does this feedback focus on? What is it about? Not the products and services, right? It's *so* not about the products and services that after 20 minutes on the phone with customers, I frequently have no idea what products or services they are buying. Why? Because it never comes up.

This feedback is about *you*.

And how you help them.

And how it *feels* to buy from you.

When your customers talk about working with you, they focus on the relationships.

And you should too.

Understand that you make your customers' lives easier by helping them in the special ways that only you can. And when you understand this, it will be much easier to do the proactive communications work that systematic organic growth requires.

PERSEVERANCE: THE ESSENTIAL MINDSET AND BEHAVIOR

Perseverance is a superpower.

Not giving up and trying again (and again) is an incredibly powerful competitive advantage.

For salespeople, perseverance is the single most important mindset *and* behavior (it is both— more on this below). Nothing else comes close. It is a singularly powerful multiplier. Consistent perseverance will make a salesperson rich.

But systematizing perseverance for your sales organization will put you so far ahead of your competition that they will never be able to catch up. If you can help your customer-facing people quickly plan and regularly apply perseverance to their opportunities, you will simply outperform every other company in your market. Because they, most likely, are *not* systematically persevering.

Why Perseverance Is So Valuable

One day I was sitting in a small professional audience when the founder of the field of positive psychology, Martin Seligman, was speaking onstage and he said something that changed my life: "Our research shows that perseverance is twice as important as talent is when it comes to success." Or, in other words, perseverance is two-thirds of the equation to success, while talent is just one-third. Read those last two sentences again, because this is mind-blowing stuff for sales teams.

Simply continuing to try is the single most important thing we can do in the sales profession, while giving up is the single most damaging thing we can do. That's why I say that perseverance is a superpower. Because most people stop. And when you continue trying, you are moving beyond your competition. You are literally showing your customers you care more, and that earning their business is important enough to you to continue trying to help. That's an incredibly powerful position to be in.

Customers can feel this, and they appreciate it. My clients frequently hear, for example, that they are the only ones following up on this quote or proposal. "Nobody else must be interested," they say with wonder. Of course, the others *are* interested; they're just too afraid to follow up because they are likely to get rejected.

Multiple top executives of larger companies—those in the hundreds of millions of dollars in revenue—have told me that when a salesperson doesn't give up and tries repeatedly to sell to them, they feel *obligated* to buy from them! That's pretty amazing, isn't it? "He's trying so hard, I feel like I owe him," they say.

The 10-Year Sale

As I write this, I just closed a significant new piece of business for a revenue growth consulting project that I've been trying to sell for more than 10 years. My previous record was four years. Ironically, both companies are in the same wholesale distribution industry. But I was open about this with my new client when he was still a prospect. We laugh about it now, and we both admire the process we went through together to get to this point of working together.

As I look back at my best and closest clients, nearly all of them told me no before they told me yes. If I had stopped trying, I simply wouldn't be working with them. Some of them I've been with for many years. I would have missed out on so much—the business, the experience, the amazing learning, and the personal relationships—if I didn't systematically implement perseverance in my work and life.

Perseverance in My Life

I started my first business during that first year of the doctoral psychology program, and I've been in business ever since. I've actually never had a job, or a boss, or a paycheck every two weeks. I see these as mostly positives, but as a result, through different economies and even during Covid (when meetings and gatherings, which are at the core of my work, vanished), we have had some very lean times.

In fact, multiple times in our lives together, my wife and I have been out of money. All the way out of money. So I learned how to persevere for a living in these desperate times. There was no choice but to keep going, despite the depression and anxiety that I felt. It was perseverance that got me out of very difficult times, repeatedly. I've said this already, but it's worth repeating: when success depends on selling, there is nothing more powerful, beneficial, and difference-making than not giving up and continuing to try.

Macro and Micro Perseverance

Like athletes, every salesperson goes through slumps. They have runs of tremendous success and then long runs of failure. This is because their success depends on other people's decisions. That is, they can do everything right and *still* not get the business. It's not up to them.

Most of my business years feature a fairly extended slump, and, usually much later, an extended period of great success. I have sometimes felt like the difficult times will never end, especially when the 12th consecutive prospect rejects working with me. But I stay focused on past experiences and the fact that the difficult times have always ended.

That's macro perseverance—it occurs over extended periods of time. There is also micro perseverance, the kind used *within* a single sale that requires executing multiple efforts or overcoming multiple rejections.

As long as I continue to do the right things (showing up, following up, being proactive)—even when they are not generating results—the slumps have always ended. As long as I've stayed in the arena . . .

Staying in the Arena

Most people have heard the line about the man in the arena. But where does it come from? Here is the full quote from Theodore Roosevelt, delivered in a speech at the Sorbonne in Paris, France, on April 23, 1910.

> *It is not the critic who counts; not the man who points out how the strong man stumbles, or where the doer of deeds could have done them better. The credit belongs to the man who is actually in the arena, whose face is marred by dust and sweat and blood; who strives valiantly; who errs, who comes short again and again, because there is no effort without error and shortcoming; but who does actually strive to do the deeds; who knows great enthusiasms, the great devotions; who spends himself in a worthy cause; who at the best knows in the end the triumph of high achievement, and who at the worst, if he fails, at least fails while daring greatly, so that his place shall never be with those cold and timid souls who neither know victory nor defeat.*

Salespeople experience mostly defeat. The best salespeople among us get eight or nine rejections for every success. But these defeats aren't always arranged so neatly in between victories: staying in the arena for eight or nine defeats is easier to handle than when they stack up, and we get 50 or 100 consecutive defeats. *This* is where hanging in there and continuing to communicate, showing up, and following up separates the most successful salespeople from everyone else.

During the difficult times, whether they last for days or many months, salespeople must stay active, stay present with customers, stay in the arena, and give themselves an opportunity to turn things around and reach success. If they quit—if they exit the arena—which is the default instinct, there will be no chance for success. There will be no more sales closed for them.

Leaders, keeping your team in the arena is your job.

How to Systematize Perseverance

The good news is that after hundreds of revenue growth projects with clients, I have learned that, like optimism, perseverance can be both learned and systematized for sales teams by business owners. Here is how:

1. Regularly share perseverance success stories your sales team has submitted. These will come to you in the Outgrow Tracking Form (OTF) and Success of the Week submissions (much more on both of these in chapter 7). Put them in front of the team. Emphasize the role that perseverance played in each sales success. Let the salespeople tell their peers their perseverance stories. By doing so you are teaching them how to not give up, and you are showing how continuing to try led directly to each sale.

2. Review opportunities that require continued efforts and follow-ups in your Monday Outgrow Huddles. Make a list of the Top 10 Perseverance Opportunities for the company and share it publicly.

3. In your Outgrow Monthly Reviews with each participant, ask them which deals they are working on that require perseverance. Ask each individual to identify their Top 5 Personal Perseverance Opportunities. Check in with them about these at the next Monthly Review.

4. You might consider incentivizing perseverance. For example, if a sale took 10 more efforts from the salesperson, or the salesperson overcame five or more rejections, they can be rewarded in some way (in addition, of course, to being recognized in the business, as in #1).

Perseverance is both an individual mindset and a critical part of an Outgrow company's culture. It begins with being regularly exposed to the positive feelings of happy customers, and then gets cemented with the success that sustained proactivity brings. The best part: Outgrow gives you a method for *systematizing perseverance* so your customer-facing people keep trying to help more customers, with more products and services. In turn, these customers will thank you with their money.

OUTGROW CASE STUDY: 76% MORE SALES OVERNIGHT

This case study is about an individual salesperson who implements Outgrow actions in his job. His name is Sam and he started Outgrow selling in October of 2022. At that time, he was an inside salesperson for J&B Supply—an Arkansas wholesale distributor of plumbing and HVAC products—generating monthly sales that were exactly the company average for his job role.

76% More Sales

When he started implementing Outgrow, his sales jumped by 76% immediately. He asked me not to use the actual sales numbers, but his numbers kept climbing, month after month.

"It was pretty instantaneous," he said. "In fact, I remember the day we did our Outgrow Launch Workshop, you had us make some proactive calls during the break. I left one of my customers and followed it with a text message like you teach. [This simple process is described in detail in chapter 7.] The customer called me back later that afternoon and gave me a big long list of stuff he needed, and he wasn't even a regular customer for us."

And it was off to the races for Sam.

"It doesn't always translate into big sales, but that little stuff adds up. I've noticed it reminds customers that we are here, and that we want to serve them. It has been a really good thing for me, because the competition around here isn't this."

The Most Effective Technique

I asked him which Outgrow technique is most effective for him.

He didn't hesitate: "The biggest one for me has been the quote follow up. At first, customers were shocked when I called them to ask if they wanted to place the order for a quote, because nobody they work with does that. Now they aren't surprised anymore when I follow up."

I asked him how he would describe Outgrow to somebody who isn't doing it yet.

"I would say it's really just taking care of my customers. But it's not in a salesy type of way. It's more me calling them to say hi, we're here if you need us. And they always need us!"

A Promotion and Employee of the Year!

Recently, Sam was promoted from his inside sales position to lead purchasing for J&B Supply.

"The Outgrow work 100% helped lead to my promotion! A few months after I started implementing Outgrow, I ended up getting Employee of the Year, and a big reason for that was Outgrow. So I have a very big appreciation for it!"

Congratulations, and go Sam go!

Chapter 3

THE STAFF PARTICIPANTS

OUTGROW ROLES AND RESPONSIBILITIES IN YOUR COMPANY

This chapter will discuss the various job roles in the Outgrow system of sales growth. Of course, each company is set up differently, with varying job titles, so I will try to be as inclusive as possible, adding alternate job titles where possible. Let's begin with staff size.

THE FIVE OUTGROW ROLES

Basically, there are five major roles in companies running Outgrow. If your firm is large enough to support the structure laid out here, it is ideal. If you are a smaller company, simply consolidate as needed, and see the support program I've built for small and solo firms at the end of this chapter. Consolidating and modifying Outgrow for your specific needs is a normal part of running this system.

1. The **owner or chief executive** is the leader of the implementation and the head coach of its execution.

2. If your company is large enough, there is one executive at the next level—think **chief operating officer, general manager, vice president, or head of sales** (if this role is at the level immediately beneath the owner or chief executive)—who should be a chief implementer. If the company is under 10 people, or less than $5 million in total revenue, this person is the same as the owner or top executive. These people are the offensive coordinators because Outgrow work is, in essence, putting your organization systematically on offense.

3. **An administrative person** who processes the inputs and outputs, and is in charge of the scorecards and success stories. Ideally, this should not be done by the executives in the two roles listed above.

4. **Managers and team leaders** who oversee the buy-in, accountability, and run the weekly Outgrow system with their teams.

5. The **frontline customer-facing people** making the communications: outside sales, inside sales, customer service, and any other groups you'd like to include.

Let's take a deeper dive into each of the Outgrow areas of responsibility:

Owner or CEO

You are the head coach. You are the owner and chief energy infuser of this initiative. Your work is to lead Outgrow, by showing your organization that it is important to you.

- Talk about it regularly with the people managing and implementing the work at all levels of your company.

- Weekly, review scorecards and success stories sent to you by the Outgrow Administrator (see below) and comment on them for the entire company.

- An Outgrow Weekly Huddle (OWH) should discuss data trends with your team: Are overall Outgrow actions increasing or decreasing? What does this mean for your near-term and long-term sales? What adjustments need to be made?

- This weekly update can review business trends in the company: What are sales doing? How is inventory? What should your staff know about market trends?

- Generate buy-in and participation with your group leaders.

- Reply to all on emails and congratulate some team members by name for their good Outgrow work.

- Pat a coworker on their back in person, thanking them for what they're doing.

- Comment on scorecards. Congratulate the people at the top, and ask the people at the bottom to dig their way out.

- Emphasize a success story to the organization. Reply privately to individuals making submissions.

- Analyze what you're seeing and hearing as leader, from your team as well as from customers and prospects.

Additionally, you will meet with your direct reports who are running Outgrow with their teams monthly. These check-ins are described in chapter 8.

Group Leaders: The General Managers, Regional Managers, Vice Presidents

These are your offensive coordinators.

- They organize and manage their next-level managers and/or frontline people (see team managers below).

- They conduct Monthly Review and Quarterly Planning Meetings with their teams.

- They monitor data and bring trends, progress, and problems to their teams' attention.

- They take direction from you, the owner or top executive, and bring it to their people.

- They generate buy-in and participation from their managers or frontline people.

Administrator

Continuing the sports metaphor, this is your analytics manager. Their role is to:

- Create, maintain, and share Outgrow action data scorecards with leadership.

- Process Outgrow success stories that have been submitted by customer-facing staff, collate them, and serve them up to leadership.

An office manager or executive assistant is the right person for this work. It would help if they are well-versed in Microsoft Excel, Google Sheets, or another number-crunching software of your choice. This is because most of the scorecard analytics work is done in a spreadsheet. If your administrator is not comfortable with spreadsheets, then the initial number crunching should be set up by a technical person, likely working in IT, and then handed off to your administrator.

Team Managers

These are your position coaches. They work closely with their individual team members to ensure the work is being done and logged. Their work is to:

- Ensure their team members understand the Outgrow actions and how to utilize them in their work.

- Make sure team members understand both how to log their actions and why it is critical to do so.

- Generate buy-in and participation from their frontline customer-facing staff.

- Lead the Monday Outgrow Huddles (or Outgrow Weekly Huddles) with their teams to review customer lists (see chapter 4) and who to communicate with. These meetings also review Outgrow action data and trends, and emphasize some key success stories from the previous week.

- Report to their managers (in the Group Leaders section above) how the Outgrow work is going with their teams.

Customer-Facing Staff

The staff members in this section are the players on the field. They are the customer-facing people taking action, being proactive, and making intentional proactive communications.

Outside Salespeople

Your outside salespeople have access to the entire playbook (laid out in chapter 6), and can implement every communication available. Their work will focus on proactive calls, quote and proposal follow-ups, and expanding the products and services your customers buy from you. If their sales require meeting the customer, managers will assign and count the activities generated by the sales meetings. If you are asking for different quantities of proactive communications from different types of salespeople, your outside people should be implementing the most proactive communications. Outside salespeople are asked to log their communications and the opportunities they create in your tracking system.

Inside Salespeople, Counter People, and Customer Service

Inside salespeople, counter workers, and customer service staff spend their days inside your office or branch, often taking orders and incoming requests. For them, the did you know questions (DYKs) and reverse did you know questions (rDYKs) will be powerful expanders of wallet share with the customers who are calling or standing in front of them. For these folks, it's important to emphasize that they can actively grow sales with people who are coming to them, whether on the phone or in person. However, although they do not need to make proactive calls to run Outgrow, most Outgrow companies do ask them for at least some outbound calls weekly. They probably have a few minutes a day to make them. Inside salespeople and customer service people are also asked to log their proactive communications and opportunities uncovered into your tracking system. If there is a line of people in front of them, or a queue on the phones, then we ask them to write down their actions and opportunities on a piece of paper and log them when there is a quiet moment.

Drivers and Technicians

If you have a logistics operation with people making deliveries, or if there are technical people on-site with customers, then nobody sees customers more than them. They are with your customers daily, and sometimes see the same people multiple times per week. But because they are not salespeople, we arm them with a simplified Outgrow approach.

Some Outgrow companies hand drivers and technicians an Outgrow card with a few bullet points on them. These can include products and services to bring up with DYK questions and language for two or three rDYK questions. The cards can rotate monthly, or even weekly, depending on which products or services you wish to emphasize.

The tracking mechanism is also simplified: we ask this group of people to simply text their actions and opportunities uncovered to their managers, or an admin, when they get back in their vehicle. The manager or admin can then log the actions into your tracking system. You can decide whether to include drivers and technicians in your reporting and scorecards. Some Outgrow companies include their success stories—and they absolutely deserve recognition, especially since it is not their job to sell—but do not include them in the scorecards. This is your call.

STAFF OR SOLO?

The Outgrow program is designed for companies with teams of people who consistently deliver proactive communications to customers. Licensed and certified Outgrow Advisors are carefully trained to help you.

However, if you are a solo provider like I've been, I have good news: Outgrow will still work extremely well for you. I was a solo consultant for over 20 years. I became the top grossing true solo consultant in the country (at least that I could find—and I tried really hard to find people who have grown a larger business than I have so that I could learn from them). My business grew exclusively by using the Outgrow principles and approaches laid out in this book.

I share the following from personal experience: solo providers—which is how most bootstrap service businesses begin, and many stay that way for years—deal with all the mindset challenges and discomforts described in the previous chapter without any of the corporate support to help with it. That is, when solo providers are scared for their future, there is no product list or customer list that will be given to them to help. When the solo has been rejected and come up empty on 20 straight selling attempts, there is no manager to prop them up or teammate to commiserate with. When failure inevitably leads to feelings of depression and anxiety, they're on their own, like I was. There is no company support. It's an intensely solitary experience. So, I've built a support structure for you.

Join Me for Outgrow Solo

Here is some more good news for solo consultants and providers: I've created an Outgrow experience just for you. It's designed to give you the same accountability, planning, and communications rhythms as the corporate teams that run the system. You will work in small teams of other solo providers, and your implementation will be by an Outgrow Advisor. There is a small fee, and if you implement the proactive communications laid out in this book and in the Outgrow Solo program, you will enjoy assured, predictable, *calming* revenue growth. Head to www.RunOutgrow.com to learn more.

Outgrow Small Business

If you run a company under $1 million in revenue but would like to scale to seven figures, I've built Outgrow Small Business especially for you. You'll be placed into a cohort of owner-peers of similarly sized operations, and, led by a licensed Outgrow Advisor, you'll set up and implement your firm's proactive, predictable revenue growth system.

OUTGROW CASE STUDY:
THE IMPLEMENTATION LEADER SEAT

Zip-O-Log Mills is a fourth-generation family sawmill business in Eugene, Oregon. I am including their story here for two interesting reasons. First, they have been running Outgrow on and off for nine years, with a gap of several years in between.

In their first round with this work, the launch of the program went quite well, and they were seeing proactive actions leading to new opportunities and sales growth. The problem was that the owner and president, Karl Hallstrom, was trying to manage the process on his own. Of course, he was very busy running the entire organization, and over time, as the business grew, his capacity to oversee Outgrow diminished, and with it, so did the Outgrow results.

Several years passed, and Karl launched a start-up called Zip-O-Laminators. He wanted to aggressively grow the new company and reintegrate the work at the original business as well. Enter his daughter KayCee Hallstrom, who took over as the implementation leader of Outgrow. With KayCee's oversight and management of Outgrow details, Zip-O's organic sales growth flourished.

Here's how Karl described results: "During the first six months that KayCee has managed this program, we've seen our sales jump about 40% at Zip-O-Laminators. We implemented some of the simple things you've taught us over the years. We made the phone calls, interacted with customers, and it's working."

Karl added: "It makes our salespeople more accountable; it keeps them on task. They're not just out there wandering around on their own—they have some direction. It's simpler than you think it is. That's not to say it's easy. It's something you have to monitor and you have to have your people do. But I think it's effective. All these calls and contacts—there's no way they're going to hurt anything."

KayCee implemented the Outgrow Tracking Form (OTF), as well as detailed reporting. Here is an example, which shows actions for those first six months. You can see that she assigned over 10,000 target Outgrow actions over that six-month period, but her team delivered 14,450 total actions in that time. That's a whopping 136% to goal.

OUTGROW SALES TRANSFORMATION INITIATIVE

Location: Eugene, OR
Total Salespeople: 4
% Participation: 100%

Client of Alex since 2016
Latest update: 05-2021

Action Summary–Assigned vs. Submitted

Total Assigned Actions since 5-1-2021:	10,594
Average Assigned Actions per Month	662
Average Assigned Actions per Week	1,661
Average Assigned Actions per Salesperson per Week	41
Total Submitted Actions since 5-1-2021:	14,450 — 36%
Average Submitted Actions per Month	903
Average Submitted Actions per Week	226
Average Submitted Actions per Salesperson per Week	56

Top 6 Actions Submitted	
1. Proactive Call	16%
2. Reverse Did You Know	16%
3. Pivot to Sale	14%
4. Did You Know	13%
5. Call When Emailed	12%
6. Quote Follow-up	11%

"The impact of your program we have implemented at Zip-O has changed the face of how we do sales," KayCee told me. "Now they have expectations. The results have been very profound at Zip-O—it has created a procedure, process, checklist, to help people be accountable. Swings and efforts mean more to me than actual sales, because the more you swing and the more confident you get, the more sales will hit. *We're in control of our swings, but sales are not in our control."*

She went on: "It really helps our salespeople. It shows how they can reach out. It shows them how they can be different. We have a long history that can show people how effective these actions are. It has been a real eye-opener for our sales staff. Especially with the customer testimonials. They can see why these customers are choosing us. That has been really important to changing our mentality. Our salespeople realized our customers want to hear from them. Changing that little bit of thinking, I saw a change in their behavior. "People *want to* hear from me. They *need to* get the product from us."

The other interesting aspect of the Outgrow effort at Zip-O is that the company employs just four salespeople and these proactive communications work just as well for this firm as they do for a company with hundreds of Outgrowers.

Outgrow works with one-person companies, four-person sales groups, and dozens, hundreds, and thousands. Outgrow is proactive organic revenue growth, scaled up or down.

Chapter 4

THE CUSTOMERS

THE REVENUE POWER OF OUTGROW CUSTOMER LISTS AND HOW TO BUILD THEM

One of the most surprising and strongest competitive advantages Outgrow companies have is a collection of detailed, organized, revenue-producing customer lists. I'm not talking about your address book, which is a collection of names, phone numbers, and emails. Nearly every company and individual salesperson has a version of this. But that list is simply an alphabetical pile of names and contact information—it doesn't help you grow your revenue.

Conversely, Outgrow Lists are built for the sole purpose of predictably growing your sales. They organize your customers into powerful groups based on the following major categories: (1) their actual revenue activity with you, (2) their future revenue or growth potential, (3) their position inside your pipeline, or (4) the length of time since you've last spoken with them.

This chapter focuses on building your Outgrow Lists and only just touches on how to approach them. Chapter 6 gets into the details of scripting and what to say to the customers and prospects on these lists when you talk with them.

WHY MOST COMPANIES DON'T HAVE THESE LISTS

These lists seem like an obvious tool every firm should have, right? Here's the thing: all companies *can* create these kinds of growth lists, but very few actually do. Why?

- It requires proactive attention and, as discussed at length, nearly all of your competition is reactive.

- It takes some time to sift through your customer records to pull these lists together, and most firms do not give it the time it requires.

- These customer records are rarely all in one place. To come up with a single list, you may have to go to your accounting software, your emails, and, perhaps, your text messages.

- Sometimes it takes multiple people to create a list: leaders, managers, and salespeople may need to discuss together who gets added to various lists. I'll detail this process in chapter 9.

- Most companies don't think of their customers in these categories.

WHAT THESE LISTS ARE USED FOR

What happens to the people on these lists? It's very simple. They get pro-active communications—usually calls and texts—from your customer-facing people.

Outgrow List Name	Definition or Details
Zero Dark 30	Customer who averaged a certain dollar amount, but little to no revenue in the last month.
Revenue Autopilot	Customers with flat monthly or annual spending, but room for increase.
Decreasing Annual Revenue	Customers spending less, year over year.
Customers Who Used to Buy, But Stopped	Business likely moved elsewhere.
Customers with Quotes or Proposals Outstanding	Quote or Proposal Follow-Up Required!
Customers Pre-Quote or Proposal	Opportunity has been opened, but not quote or proposal. Pre-quote / proposal follow-up required to get to pricing.
Large Customers Who Can Buy More	Your biggest and best, but the rDYK will lead to even more.
Small and Medium Customers Who Can Buy More	They are probably not hearing much from your team today. The rDYK (what else?) will work wonders here.
Prospective Customers Who Did Not Buy	You know each other and have a relationship. Go back to them.
Prospective Customers You Haven't Talked To (Cold)	Not a customer yet, but they are probably buying from your competition.
Customers You Haven't Talked to in Six Months or More	Powerful group to call proactively, easy business here.

You and your leaders will discuss the lists with your managers, and they will review the customers with frontline staff in your Monthly Review meetings and your Outgrow Weekly Huddles. Managers will then assign a target number of customers from specific lists to receive phone calls and other communications.

These lists are a gold mine for revenue growth. Your customer-facing staff will never have to wonder who they should call each day. These Outgrow Customer Lists help you steer the ship of your company, directly toward significant sales growth. Best part: the more customers are contacted on these lists, the more your sales will grow.

The chart on the previous page shows an inclusive Outgrow List of Lists, which can be downloaded in its most updated entirety at www .RunOutgrow.com.

Please note that the lists that appear here have some overlap. They are not designed to be totally unique from each other. Rather, they are designed to help you think of as many people as possible to sell to. Can a name appear on multiple lists? Sure. Do you need to worry about adding names to their exactly correct list? Absolutely not. Just think of people, write them down, and then we'll go proactively communicate with them.

LISTS BASED ON CUSTOMER REVENUE ACTIVITY

This first set of customer lists is based on changes in their dollars spent with you. Specifically, these customers are either spending less with you or are consistently level.

Zero Dark 30 Customers

This is a list category a large regional wholesale distribution client of mine came up with recently. I give them credit for the list, but I am pleased to be the one who named it, in honor of the tremendous movie. This list consists of customers who average a certain annual dollar amount with you—in my client's case, the cutoff was $10,000 spent annually—but no sales in the last 30 days.

So, they're large enough to be interesting—you decide what that means, annually—but there has been no revenue in the last month. Why could this be? In my experience, these customers have likely moved their business elsewhere. They probably haven't stopped buying altogether, since they typically need the product or service to do their work. So, quietly, they've probably taken their business somewhere else.

When your people call the customers on this list, they can say, "I notice we haven't been helping you over the last month as usual. It's important to me to help you. What do you have coming up that we can assist with?" This is incredibly compelling to the customer because: (1) you noticed—this is a *big* deal for customers!—and (2) you communicated to say you're ready to assist again.

As a result, it has been my clients' experience that the great majority of the customers on this list either buy something immediately on the call or shortly thereafter.

Customers on Revenue Autopilot

This is a list of customers who buy the same products and services regularly. Their monthly or annual spend is consistent, within a narrow maximum and minimum band. They buy what they buy, and your salespeople sell what they ask for without attempting to expand on it. For years.

But then, if we step beyond this narrow, niched buying, there are so many other products and services you can help them with. It's probable they are buying things from your competition that they could—and *should*—be buying from you. Who are these customers?

You find them by running a report in your accounting software, or wherever you track customers' monthly or annual spend. You're looking for people who are plus or minus 10% to 20% consistently, but never more or less. Your salespeople will go to them and ask to help them more. They will ask, "What else do you buy that I can help you with?" And then you will experience what so many of my Outgrow clients enjoy: your customers will accept your offer and they will buy more—this time, and then repeatedly in the future.

Customers with Decreasing Annual Revenue

This list contains customers who are spending less, year over year. It's possible the revenue in *their* business is decreasing, but it's far more likely that they've moved purchasing they used to do with you to another firm. This is very difficult to notice, unless you are actively looking for it. Customers probably don't call you to tell you they are moving some of their business to someone else.

Why is this happening? Perhaps your competitor called and asked for additional business. This is rare, as I've said, but it does happen. Perhaps your customer was driving to his or her customer, needed some product for the job, and noticed another supplier on the way. Or maybe your customer had lunch with this other person and their working relationship expanded as a result.

Your salespeople and customer service people can call these customers and say something like this: "I couldn't help but notice our work together is decreasing. It's important to me to make sure you're getting what you need from us. What are you buying elsewhere that I can help you with?" This is an rDYK.

They will tell you because most people are shocked and impressed that your frontline person is asking such a direct and incredibly helpful question. People always want to be helped more—it's a fact of life. This communication stems from your staff noticing they've actually been helping these customers *less* and asking to help them some more. Many customers will accept because it will make their lives easier.

Customer Who Used to Buy but Stopped

This is a list of customers who used to buy from you, but they stopped entirely. For these people, unless they retired or went out of business, they didn't stop buying what you sold them; they simply stopped buying it from you. In this case, they continue to buy it elsewhere.

Although the list itself is straightforward, compiling it requires going into your accounting software and searching for customers who used to do business with you, but their sales have dropped to zero. Without actively searching for them, it's very difficult to even know that these customers have gone away. They don't call to break up with you, right? They simply go away, quietly. We almost never notice it. And so, finding them, like the other customer types already detailed, requires a bit of intentional focus and effort.

What do your people say to these customers? Something like this: "Hi, Tom, I know we haven't done much business lately, but I was thinking of you because another customer I was working with reminded me of you." Or, "Hi, Tom, I couldn't help but notice you haven't purchased X, Y, and Z for some time like you used to. I'd sure love to help you with that again."

LISTS BASED ON CUSTOMER PIPELINE POSITION

These next four lists are based on your customers' position in your pipeline. They are either pre- or post-quote (or proposal), or they've already purchased and there is opportunity for them to buy additional products and services.

Please note, there is some overlap here, especially with some of the lists above. It's perfectly normal for customers to appear in more than one Outgrow Customer List. If your database allows for tagging or categorizing customers, these lists are easy to create. We'll talk more about using these tools toward the end of this chapter.

Customers with Outstanding Quotes or Proposals

A simple but extremely valuable list, these are customers who have an outstanding quote or proposal from you. They require a follow-up to close the business. This list will help your salespeople know who needs a quote or proposal follow-up. This communication is described at length in chapter 6, so I won't go into much detail here other than to share the basic language: "Hi, Tom, I was thinking about you. Where are you on that quote? I'd love to help you with that."

Some of my clients give their salespeople their list of outstanding quotes and proposals before they head out on the road to see customers. If you're comfortable with making calls during driving (and I certainly am), they can simply move through the list and make their quote follow-up calls while they drive to see their customers.

In theory, these customers with quotes and proposals should be easier to remember, right? *Why do they need a list?*, you might be thinking. Well, depending on your type of company, the large and most interesting quotes and proposals tend to be the ones that are remembered. The mid-size ones tend not to stick in our memories. The smaller ones are usually very difficult to recall, even a day or two after they are issued.

I am constantly surprised what a tiny percentage of quotes and proposals receive a follow-up. Usually it's because your salespeople forget since they are so busy reacting to customer issues. This list will help your people remember and actively express interest in helping your customers with what has been quoted and proposed.

Customers with Pending Opportunities (Pre-Quote/Pre-Proposal)

What about those customers that are *pre-quote or pre-proposal?* There is a live opportunity that your staff has discussed with them, but it is too soon for the quote or proposal. Where do these customers live? On this list!

The quote or proposal follow-up attempts to move customers toward closing the business. But a pre-quote or pre-proposal follow-up tries to move your customers toward the quote or proposal. It typically goes something like, "Are you ready for that quote? I'd love to help you with that." It moves the deal along in your pipeline.

Getting this list together is harder than some of the others because the opportunity often does not exist anywhere besides your salesperson's mind. If there is no central customer relationship management software, this list is a challenge. And even if there is a CRM, I hardly know any companies that are full of salespeople who are using their CRM perfectly, making this list very difficult to gather.

For Outgrow companies, this list is usually built during the Outgrow Weekly Huddles, when your team gathers to discuss proactive opportunities. This is the perfect time to talk about what opportunities are on the table and who needs to be prompted to move toward a quote or proposal.

Large Customers Who Can Buy More

This list contains your best customers who account for the biggest percentage of your revenue. But not all of them are buying everything they need from you. Some might be, but some certainly are not. Which ones can buy even more? This list can only be made through discussion among the customer-facing team and leadership who serve these customers, because qualification is determined by knowledge and experience with each individual customer. It requires the people at your firm who know each customer to put their heads together.

When your people call these folks, they can ask a simple rDYK question: "I know we do a lot of work together, but I was wondering, what else do you have going on that I'm not helping you with?"

At the end of this chapter, I will take you through a planning exercise to help you determine your highest-growth-potential customers.

Small to Medium Revenue Customers Who Can Buy More

Now, consider your small and midsize customers. Which ones can buy significantly more than they are currently? Most salespeople are usually spending a lot of time with their largest customers, as well as the customers making incoming inquiries and requests, but *the great majority of small to midsize customers are probably not hearing much from your company.* This list will help your people know who they are and go to them.

Like the previous list of your largest customers, you'll need to coordinate with your customer-facing teams to determine which of your small to medium customers have the greatest opportunity to increase their spending with you. These are the ones we are interested in communicating with.

These calls will sound something like, "Tom, we love doing business with you—what percent of your business would you guess we have? I'd sure value a shot at helping you with the work we're not getting today." This is called the percent of business question, and it's covered in detail in chapter 6.

PROSPECTS WHO HAVE NEVER BEEN CUSTOMERS

Now let's look at prospective customers with whom you have not yet done any business. There are two types of prospective customers: those you've talked to and those you haven't yet talked to. There is a universe of potential customers in each group. The key is narrowing them down to the best and most interesting ones. That's what the next two lists focus on.

Prospective Customers You've Talked to Who Did Not Buy

My universe is full of these prospects. We talked about a project together, but they did not buy. Possibly, they saw me live in person as a speaker. After that, we spoke on the phone, possibly multiple times. Then we may have even had an in-person meeting. And they may have even gotten a proposal from me. This is my general pipeline. If at any point in this process a prospect said "no" or removed themselves from the process, they are a past prospect to me.

This is an incredibly important group of people in my business—and probably in yours. They know you, and they know your people. They know how you work, the products you carry, and the services you deliver. *They are fairly familiar with the advantages of doing business with you.* When you reach out to these past prospects—even if it has been years since you last communicated—you are not starting from zero. In fact, you are starting approximately 50% toward the closed sale. There is a history and foundation.

Some of these past prospects can immediately become a medium or large customer at your firm. But they are difficult to track down because there is probably not an existing central list of them. In fact, they probably mostly exist in the emails, text messages, sales notes (often on paper), and faded memories of your salespeople. Determine what systems these people's names can be found in, and go to them. Spend the time that putting this list together requires.

Because there is a lot of opportunity in this list.

Your language at the start of a call here goes something like this: "I can't believe it has been a year since we last spoke. How have you been? I was thinking about you, as I've been helping my clients during this slower economy. How is the economy affecting your business? Should we revisit our conversation now that the environment has changed?" Of course, *any* reason to try to help them again is a good reason. And it doesn't have to be a year—a week, a month, or five years are perfectly good lengths of time to go back to past prospects with your tremendous value.

Prospective Customers You Have Not Talked To—Who Are Buying from Your Competition

This is a list of potential customers whom your organization is aware of, but they are not buying from you currently. You have not interacted before. And because they buy the products and services that you sell, it's safe to presume that they are buying from your competition. So, you know who this customer is, because they are significant enough to be on your radar, and they may or may not know that your firm is able to help them.

Because your various salespeople and managers have knowledge of different prospective customers like this, putting this list together requires a team conversation with phones and laptops open. This is a pro-active (there's that word again) back-and-forth exchange to build this list. You cannot build a list like this without actively and intentionally making time for it. It doesn't build itself.

When your salespeople call these prospects, the conversation begins with, "I know you are with X Competitor currently, but I'm aware of your work and reputation in the industry and I wanted to reach out to learn more and try to earn your business. I'd be grateful for the opportunity."

CUSTOMERS YOU HAVEN'T TALKED TO IN SIX MONTHS OR MORE

This is a group so large and important that it gets its own stand-alone category. It also includes customers on a number of the lists we've already reviewed. However, Outgrow salespeople find it easy and useful to think of customers in terms of how long it's been since they've spoken with them.

You might be surprised that more than half of your company's accounts may fall in this category. But, amazingly, when asked directly, most salespeople cannot think of five customers they haven't talked to in six months. That's because these customers are not on their minds; they don't talk to them. And, almost certainly, the customers aren't thinking very much about your (their) salesperson either. To be clear: this list focuses on conversations in person or on the phone. Emails don't count because they are basically useless in growing sales. They are useful for taking and fulfilling orders, but they do nothing for *expanding* orders and growing wallet share.

So, sit with your people during your Outgrow Weekly Huddles and ask them to go to their address book apps, and their emails, and their old text messages. Ask them, at the table, to list 5 to 10 customers they haven't talked to in six months or more. Then, ask them to reach out to these folks this week to say, "I know it has been a while since we've last talked, but I was thinking about you and hoping everything was going well. What are you working on that I might be able to help with?"

FINER POINTS ABOUT OUTGROW LISTS

Now that we have gone through all of the customer lists, here are seven quick finer points about them.

You Don't Need Perfect Lists; You Just Need Lists

I frequently say to Outgrow salespeople that you don't need to call the perfect customer; you just need to call some customers and ask to help them more. Just as you don't need to offer the perfect did-you-know product or service—you simply need to offer some products or services that they aren't buying today but that you think will be helpful to them. So, take the pressure of perfection off yourself. The lists don't need to be perfect. They are living and developing, just as your business is.

You Don't Need All the Lists; You Just Need Some Lists

This chapter contains nine customer lists and two prospect lists. You don't need all of them. You might aspire to get to all of them eventually. But, frankly, three different customer lists are enough here—build yourself the "six months or more" list, plus two additional customer lists you can easily and quickly put together, and go to work. Enlist the help of your leaders, managers, and salespeople.

Starting to communicate with the people on the lists is the most important thing. Don't allow the list building to get in the way of that.

List Names of Humans and Companies

Frequently, unless I specifically indicate to include the names of the people who are your customers and prospects, my clients will build lists consisting solely of company names. We sell to people. And, critically, there are often multiple buyers and influencers within a customer company. So, as you lead your staff through building your Outgrow Lists, focus them on the names of the people they have relationships with and the ones they wish to develop them with.

Customers Can Be on Multiple Lists

I've mentioned this within the lists, but it's worth repeating here in its own space: if these lists are built correctly, customers will appear on multiple lists. As an example, the same customer might be a smaller customer who can buy a lot more and a customer whose revenue is decreasing and someone you haven't talked to in six months or more. It's helpful to think of people from different perspectives—what their revenue activity is doing, their position on your pipeline, or the length of time since you've talked with them. Thinking about customers this way helps you think of and find more customers to proactively call. And that's the goal.

The Lists Are Updated Regularly

The lists are living, breathing, and changing, representing the current moment in time. For example, the Zero Dark 30 list—which contains customers who have done some significant revenue with you annually, but none in the last month—updates every 30 days, with some customers falling off and some coming on. Some of the lists are able to be automatically updated. Others require proactive discussion and periodic manual updating. How they're updated almost doesn't matter. What matters is that your customer-facing staff has Outgrow Customer Lists full of customers to intentionally communicate with and predictably grow your sales.

Proactive Discussions with Your Team Are the Key to Building Outgrow Lists

The Outgrow Quarterly Meetings, Monthly Reviews, and Weekly Huddles are your key points of connection with your team to build these lists. The more customer-facing staff can lend their knowledge and experiences with your buyers and prospects, the better and longer your lists will be.

Critically, it doesn't require hours or even an hour. Carving out a small portion of your Outgrow interactions toward list building is enough. Why is such a short amount of time enough? Because when people's minds are in a proactive state, constructive and even creative work happens easily and quickly. Bring them in, focus them on "who else" should be hearing from us, go around the room, and you will find results come quickly. I cover all the steps of these meetings in chapter 8.

WHAT MAKES THE OUTGROW CUSTOMER LISTS SO VALUABLE?

Here are the top three reasons that customer lists are so valuable.

1. **Your Staff Never Has to Wonder Who to Call:** When you ask people to implement a behavior that is naturally uncomfortable, like making a proactive call, not knowing who to call is a major obstacle. These customer lists remove that obstacle. Your people will always have an array of customers and prospects, listed in

black and white, who they can reach out to, catch up with, and ask, *What else?*

2. **You Will Gain Powerful Insights:** Even if no additional business is added, and even if no new opportunities are opened, you will learn valuable insights about the customers you are calling. These can include:

    -   What else this customer has coming up in the near future
    -   Why this customer is not currently doing more business with you
    -   Why the customer *is* buying from you
    -   What other companies the customer buys from
    -   When the next selling opportunity is expected
    -   How your pricing stacks up against the competition

    There is only upside to learning these details.

3. **Outgrow Lists Are a Road Map for Sales Growth:** Outgrow Customer Lists are filled with dozens, maybe hundreds, of people who you can help more. As such, they are growth lists. These lists offer stability for your firm and your people. They calm nerves and soothe anxieties. They show you exactly who will bring more revenue to your organization. And that's a heck of a competitive advantage to have.

4. **Outgrow Lists Let You Be Prescriptive:** As your company's leader, these lists will help you steer your company toward specific kinds of growth. For example, you will be able to say to your salespeople, "This week, call five customers on the Decreasing Annual Revenue list and focus your people there." Or you might focus on the Zero Dark 30 list for a week and ask your people to dial up every customer on that list and ask what's going on that you can help with. The Outgrow Customer Lists arm you with a way to ask for specific proactive activities to be delivered to specific customers.

STUDY: THE OUTGROW EXPERIMENT

Service Professionals Don't Like to Sell

This company is a professional services firm in the engineering space. There are a few salespeople, but 90% of the Outgrowers are engineers. In this industry, engineers who are asked to develop business are called seller-doers. They uncover opportunities, write proposals, sell the services, and then deliver them. If you're a solo service provider, you are likely also a seller-doer.

The most important thing to know is that they are not salespeople. More emphatically, the prevailing mindset among many trained professional service providers—engineers, lawyers, accountants, project managers, consultants—is: *I didn't become an engineer to be a used car salesperson.* These are not people who find the selling aspect of their work attractive. That's the starting point: helping people sell who initially (1) don't want to sell, and (2) view the work as somewhat beneath them.

Two Years of Outgrow Led to 77% Growth

This is a company that has been around for 75 years, and was generating a flat (slow to no growth) $43 million per year in 2021. That year, one of its three divisions began implementing Outgrow. From 2021 to 2023, they generated 77% combined growth, with the same C-suite leadership.

One of Three Divisions Implemented Outgrow

The most interesting thing about this Outgrow organization is that they initially implemented the program in just one of their three divisions. This set up a proper experiment: we had an Outgrow group and two control groups. Division One started Outgrow in 2021 in earnest. The initiative expanded company-wide to Divisions Two and Three in mid-2023. So we have 2.5 years of Division One-on-Outgrow results to compare to the rest of the company, which was running its business as usual. All three divisions were in generally strong growth sectors. However, Division One was in somewhat slower categories—like aviation, federal government, hospitality, and K–12 education—than the control groups.

Here is the revenue breakdown:

- Division One added 143% growth.

- Divisions Two and Three, combined, added 38%.

- Division One grew 3.75 times faster than Divisions Two and Three.

- Division One was made up of four teams in 2021, and has doubled in size to eight teams today.

Why and how did this happen? The answers are laid out in the rest of this book, but here are the keys; in short:

- The seller-doers realized their clients needed more help from them.

- They started assigning a target set of weekly actions for their seller-doers to implement weekly.

- They started calling clients when nothing was wrong, regularly asking, "What other projects can we help with?"

- They followed up on proposals regularly.

- They tracked these efforts, counted them, and shared the scorecards with everyone. This instilled awareness, accountability, and some healthy competition.

- Internally, they publicly recognized the wins and successes, rewarding participants.

The president of the company told me, "Outgrow simplified and systematized our business development. We had a plan of where we wanted to go, and we used Outgrow as the scorecard to make sure everybody was doing the work. Outgrow was our tracking mechanism."

When the effort expanded to the company at large, I led their launch workshop, and as happens in all launch workshops, we listened to and debriefed audio recordings of happy clients sharing glowing reviews of the engineers they work with.

"The thing that was the most powerful was when you came to us and changed our mindset," the president explained. "You made us proud about what we were doing to help our clients."

This allowed them to go back out into the marketplace confident, bold, and enthusiastic. The mindset change is the foundation on which systematic activity is built.

The best part is, whether you are a sole proprietor, a small-but-growing firm, or a large, established organization in a mature industry, you can create this kind of intentional, organic systematic growth too. The details are in your hands. The details are in this book.

Chapter 5

THE WALLET SHARE EXPANSION

SELLING MORE PRODUCTS AND SERVICES TO YOUR CURRENT CUSTOMERS

There are three ways to expand your wallet share with current customers, and these are not mutually exclusive. You can stack, or combine, these efforts, customer by customer:

1. Expand the products and services each customer buys.

2. Increase quantity or volume of the current products you are selling to each customer.

3. Sell to additional individual buyers within each customer.

Let's examine each of these approaches.

OUTGROW WALLET SHARE EXPANDER

Customer Name: _____   Date: _____

Top Products or Services Being Purchased Today		Can They Buy More?
1.		
2.		
3.		
4.		
5.		
6.		

Additional Products or Services Likely Needed [DYK Items]
1.
2.
3.
4.
5.
6.

Additional Buyers		
Name	Role	Contact Plan [Who Will Intro You?]
1.		
2.		
3.		
4.		
5.		
6.		

EXPANDING WHICH PRODUCTS AND SERVICES YOUR CUSTOMERS BUY

It is my experience with more than 400 clients and tens of thousands of salespeople who have implemented Outgrow that your typical customers are *maybe* consciously aware of about 20% of everything they can buy from you. But this number is probably lower, and actually limited to the products and services they already buy from you. Meanwhile, they go elsewhere, to your competition, to buy the various other products and services they need. Imagine if they knew about 30% of your total offerings instead of just 20%—the focus is on systematically expanding your customers' awareness of how you can help them.

Customers Niche You, and You Niche Them

An Outgrow salesperson shared this story with his colleagues in a meeting I was facilitating: "I was with one of my biggest customers, who has been buying the same few products from us for over 15 years. Casually, he brought up needing our main product that we are known for and having trouble finding it. I told him I can totally supply that for him. He . . . was . . . stunned. And I was shocked. He's one of my best customers, and he didn't know I could help him with our main product that everybody comes to us for."

How often have you and your salespeople heard this line from customers: "I didn't know you did (or had) that!" They say this even though you may have told them about this very product or service not that long ago. Maybe just a couple weeks ago. But it wasn't important to them at the time.

Similarly, your Outgrowers niche your customers right back, thinking, *My customers buy what they need. If they need something else, they'll ask me.* That's not possible because they don't *know* what else they can buy from you. How can they ask if they have no awareness of your other products?

This is why a significant part of the Outgrow effort is to un-niche how your customers and your staff view each other.

This is about your Outgrowers going to customers and telling them about other products and services they can buy from you and asking them what they buy elsewhere, which lets the customer inform your staff about what else they need.

Salespeople Notoriously Overestimate Wallet Share

Because salespeople interact at great lengths and depths with just some of their customers—usually the squeaky wheels who bring them issues and problems—they almost always overestimate how much of their customers' business they have. "Oh, they buy almost everything from us," they announce with great confidence. Then, we go to the customer and ask the percent of business question—which is exactly what it sounds like: *How much of your overall business would you estimate you give us?*— and the answers are consistently *well* below the salesperson's estimate. This communication technique will be described in more detail in the next chapter.

Here's the thing: if the salesperson believes they have the vast majority of what there is to get with their customers, they won't try to get more because they don't think it's possible. I described at length about how behavior follows mindset in chapter 2, and this is a perfect illustration of how the default sales mindset hurts your business.

So, it's important to show your salespeople that they have less of their customers' business than they think. You do this by assigning the percent of business question as a weekly action for your salespeople early on in your Outgrow implementation. (This process is described in chapter 7.) It's a surprising, sometimes painful aha moment. And the natural follow-up question is: "What else do you buy that I'm not getting?" which is an rDYK question.

Your Salespeople Probably Don't Know Everything Else You Sell

Another reason for the niching between your Outgrowers and your customers is that often salespeople don't have awareness of the entire scope of your offerings. Now, I have clients in wholesale distribution that sell 100,000 different products. I have other clients who offer just 20 or so products and services. In both cases, salespeople tend to focus on the products and services they are most comfortable with. This includes offerings they can speak in depth on and answer all questions on. This is normal human behavior: we ask about products and services that we know and have familiarity with.

Here's a key and potentially painful question: If your customer-facing staff doesn't have your products and services in their minds, how can they possibly put them into your customers' minds? And so, it's just as important to expand your Outgrowers' awareness of your various offerings as it is to educate your customers on them. Here's how to do it.

1. **Regularly distribute product and service lists.** My most successful cross-selling clients have line cards and offerings lists readily available for their Outgrowers to reference. These are simple one- or two-page bulleted lists that broadly detail your firm's products and services. This means it's more of a description of brands, lines, and product or service categories and subcategories. It's not specific parts and part numbers. There are other places to dig deeper for those.

2. **Email details about a featured product or service weekly.** Outgrow companies also regularly send an internal email featuring a weekly product or service and three to five important points about each. These are set to arrive into your customer-facing staff's inboxes on the same day each week, and can be preloaded in advance by a marketing person or an admin. You can time these to coordinate with promotions throughout the year.

3. **Create DYK lists of high-potential cross-selling products and services.** Think of these Outgrow DYK lists as a powerful collection of "if/then" lists:

DYK If/Then	
If the Customer Buys:	If the Customer Buys:
DYKs:	DYKs:
If the Customer Buys:	If the Customer Buys:
DYKs:	DYKs:

You are thinking through which additional products or services can be beneficial. So if the customer buys *this* product or service from us, they probably also need *these* additional items. Please note that the DYK items can be directly related to an item being purchased or in a completely different category. And when your people ask DYKs, it's reasonable to ask about both kinds of products: complementary ones and those in another category altogether.

These DYK lists can be created by the organization—somebody in marketing or an administrative assistant—for your Outgrowers, or you might include working through the creation of DYK lists in your Outgrow Quarterly Meetings or your Weekly Huddles. This forces your people to think through and consider your company's various offerings and how they fit together. These lists should be easily accessible as reference documents, and also actively placed in front of your people via internal emails, messages, and in conversation.

4. **Distribute rotating product or service cards for your teams.** Using the materials detailed above, my Outgrow client companies will position featured products and DYK lists directly in front of the eyes of their customer-facing staff. For inside salespeople and customer service people who work at their desks, they will tape a small card to the bottom of their monitor or place a small folded tent card on their desk with a series of bullet points with products listed to ask DYKs about.

   For outside salespeople who spend time in their cars, a similar reminder card can be placed on the dashboard or center console. Some salespeople place it inside their phone case, facing out, so they can simply turn their phone over and be reminded of products and services to ask customers about. These product and service cards rotate over time.

How to Expand the Products and Services Your Customers Buy

Here are four ways to help your customers benefit from more of your products and services.

Tell Them What Else You Offer with Did You Know Questions

The DYK is one of the simplest, most basic communications that exists in Outgrow and, frankly, the entire selling profession. The DYK simply asks customers if they knew you offered a particular product or service:

- Did you know we also offer product X?

- How are you on service Y? Do you need that as well?

- Do you need any product Z with that?

These questions take three seconds to ask, and 20% of them result in a line item being added over time. Some of the items are added immediately and others are added later when a need develops. The idea is for your Outgrowers to use the various reminder devices detailed here to constantly ask their customers about additional products and services.

Ask Them What Else They Need with Reverse Did You Know Questions

As effective as the DYK question is, the rDYK opens and closes even more business. Think of the rDYK as the "what else" question:

- What else do you need me to quote?

- What else are you buying from my competition that I can help you with?

- What else would you like me to add to our project?

In the DYK, your staff suggests the product or service. In the rDYK, the customer *tells them* exactly what they need, often naming multiple products or services. Frequently my Outgrow client salespeople get a *list* of 10 or more products to write up.

"But I only sell one product or service."

Sometimes in Outgrow workshops, a participant raises his or her hand and says, "I only sell one service."

I ask about it. What service?

Often, they say something like "information technology support."

I inquire further about how it's delivered and they explain that for a single ongoing monthly maintenance fee, they deliver *all* of their services.

If you offer everything all at once, ask yourself what can be unbundled from that package and charged for additionally. For example, for an IT company client, I ask: *Can you offer an initial audit to assess their systems? Can you separate computers from networking? Local storage from cloud storage?* If you sell products, I ask, *Can you price annual maintenance separately?* If you sell consumable products for machinery, like blades—*Can you offer regular intermittent deliveries? What about a stocking program on-site with the customer?* All of these items can make for good DYK questions.

The key with these lists is the same as the lists discussed in the previous chapter: they require some proactive time and attention to brainstorm and put together. You cannot unbundle in reactive mode, bouncing from one issue to another.

INCREASE THE QUANTITY OR VOLUME OF THE CURRENT PRODUCTS OR SERVICES YOU ARE SELLING TO EACH CUSTOMER

In addition to expanding product mix, another way to grow wallet share with existing customers is to sell more volume of the products and services you are already delivering. There are a few ways to do this:

1. The obvious one: simply sell them more. Ask if they are buying *all* of this particular product or service from you. If not, inform them you'd like to make their lives easier and service all their needs on these items all at once. With this action, you are taking business away from your competition.

2. Product companies can offer an inventory program to keep your customers' shelves stocked with products, ensuring they always have them when they need them. This is extremely valuable to customers because they never have to worry about running out

of product. In this case, your salesperson is simply counting how many units are left on the shelves and making up the difference between that and the agreed-to inventory levels.

3. Next, if you are selling products that your customers buy frequently, you can implement an automatic delivery program and make sure products are shipped on a regular basis. This is like a subscription. Amazon runs a similar program, often for a small discount, and you can even choose the intervals at which your product arrives. I will tell you that *every time* I've signed up for one of these subscriptions, I bought more product than I did with one-off purchases.

4. If you sell a service, a related approach is to schedule out your efforts throughout the year. If your firm fixes and maintains products, you might offer a preventative maintenance plan, which will have your people on-site monthly or quarterly rather than only when something goes wrong. Similarly, if you offer professional services, you can schedule monthly interactions, for example, which will likely create significantly more billing opportunities.

SELL TO ADDITIONAL INDIVIDUAL BUYERS WITHIN EACH CUSTOMER

Just as salespeople regularly overestimate how much business they do with a customer, they also frequently believe they are doing business with *every* possible individual buyer at each customer. The truth is that frequently there are additional individuals who you don't work with who can buy your products or services. For most whole distribution companies that I work with, for example, more than 75% of their customers have people who can buy from them but currently do not.

THE WALLET SHARE EXPANSION   103

I considered putting this approach into the previous chapter on customer lists, but the problem is we don't often know the names of these
additional potential buyers. So we have to ask for them. This technique is
called Internal Referral Request, and, depending on the type of company,
is a version of this simple question: "Which of your colleagues am I am
not working with?"

Here are some different types of companies, and advice for how to ask
for other potential buyers there:

1. If you sell to contractors, where each individual doing work for
    them buys from a different supply house, you can ask: "What
    other contractors do you work with who I can help the way that
    I help you?"

2. If your customers are service firms like engineers, architects,
    accountants, or lawyers, you might say, "What other people do
    you work with who I'm not helping?"

3. If your customers are very large companies with multiple
    divisions and profit centers, you can ask about them like this:
    "What other divisions are there here that I should be working
    with?"

4. If you work with interior designers, for example, you can
    specifically ask about them: "What other designers do you work
    with? I'd love to take care of them too."

A system for doing this is to sit down and make a list of customers
(there's that tool again) who *probably* have multiple others who can buy
from you. Then create your specific Internal Referral Request language
and go to each of these customers and ask your question.

OUTGROW CASE STUDY: CUSTOMIZING OUTGROW FOR DIFFERENT COMPANIES

"Outgrow creates habitual proactivity regardless of the business setting," said Ryan Hilsinger, the president of three different complementary lumber companies: East Coast Lumber, a large regional wholesale lumber distributor that sells product very quickly, often in one call; Industrial Wood Products, a wood remanufacturing facility with five large facilities that modify lumber by cutting it, regrading it, or finishing it, which has a longer sales cycle that can take weeks or months; and NC Lumber & Supply, a retail lumberyard business with 13 locations, where sales happen while the customer is in the store.

From $85M to $200M

Ryan's companies have been running Outgrow for over seven years. When they started, there were 150 total employees, 15 of whom were salespeople, and the company did $85 million in annual sales. Today, there are 300 employees, 30 salespeople, and $200 million in annual sales. That's a 20% compound annual growth rate.

"Outgrow emboldens salespeople more than anything else out there," he said. "We're not waiting for the phone to ring. We're finding new opportunities on every call that's already happening, *and* we're picking up the phone to call people to create even more opportunities."

Ryan's firms have a compensation process for salespeople: they begin with a salary while they learn how to sell lumber. As sales ramp up, compensation becomes commission only. Before Outgrow, this transition process took two years, on average. Today, it takes less than one year. "Those guys are empowered to ask about what else customers need for *this* project, and also what other projects they can help with."

Customizing the Outgrow Process for Different Companies

Ryan has an interesting implementation of Outgrow because he's using it in three very different companies, with three very different sales processes.

"We modify how we use Outgrow for each company," he explained, "and I have different levels of expectations for each organization. But it is very customizable, and we've been able to apply it for each use case very well."

At East Coast Lumber, the distribution firm, "they can buy and sell anything in the marketplace, and it happens very quickly, often on the same call." So they're asking DYKs, rDYKs, and pivoting to the sale a lot: "I have some [product] coming in—do you want me to set it aside for you?"

Ryan continues: "But at Industrial Wood Products, we are a contracting wood company, and we have to ask lots of DYKs so that our customers know about our capabilities. And at our retail business, we really have to build that sale while the customers are in our lumberyards, so we ask lots of DYKs about things like 'have you thought about doing a painted tongue-and-groove on the ceiling?' Face-to-face interaction on the sales floor can be drastically different than phone interactions."

He estimates that 50 to 75% of their growth has been a result of Outgrow. "Every salesperson, new or old, their mentality has shifted because of this program. And the new guys that come in, they don't know any different. When they step into our organization, they start Outgrow selling. They don't know there's any different way, because here, everyone is selling this way."

ABOUT THESE COMMUNICATIONS

Chapter 6

THE PROACTIVE COMMUNICATIONS

I n the previous chapters we've prepared for taking action and even introduced some of this chapter's communication techniques. We have covered the all-important Outgrow culture and mindset shifts; the team members who will grow your revenue; the customer lists and how to put them together; and finally, the three approaches to sell more products and services to your current customers. Now, it's time to define the actions. These are the tools in the toolbox we will hand to every customer-facing person on your team.

ABOUT THESE COMMUNICATIONS AND WHAT THEY HAVE IN COMMON

Here are some important big-picture details about the communications detailed in this chapter and what they have in common.

They Are All Proactive Communications

Every one of the communications listed here is proactive, meant to be utilized when there is no problem to address with your customers. Almost every other salesperson talks to your customers in response to a problem or urgency, but your people will reach out to them using these techniques outside of crisis.

This seems like an odd point to emphasize, but it's very important: *communications grow sales.* List making doesn't grow sales. Preparing scripts doesn't grow sales. Even solving your customers' problems doesn't grow sales. That action retains customers, usually, but not always, because it's totally reactive and others can come and offer lower prices and poach your customers even when you are effectively reacting to their concerns.

Communications grow sales because the more that customers hear from your team, the more they will buy. And the less they hear from your team, the less they will buy. It never works the other way: you can never communicate less and sell more. It's against the laws of physics. Consistent proactive communication is the currency with which predictable revenue growth is created.

One more thing: each of these communications is to be *spoken*, not emailed. Emails make you totally forgettable, and actually hurt the sale. Your people can certainly email customers for customer service work or problem resolution or quote delivery. But an email is never an Outgrow action.

They Are All Designed to Be Done Very Quickly

Many of the communications that follow can be delivered in just a few seconds. These include the already mentioned DYK and rDYK questions and quote follow-ups. There are others that are lightning fast.

The actions involving proactive phone calls *might* take a few minutes, if the customer picks up. Outgrower calls that connect average about four minutes in total length. But most of the time your people will reach voicemails and leaving a message takes maybe 30 seconds (and many of our scripts are faster than that).

In total, we're looking for less than five minutes a day of proactive communications from each customer-facing person. Not per customer. But per Outgrower, per day. We can round it up to 30 minutes a week of outbound communications per customer-facing person.

They Are Obvious

These are approaches that your sales and customer service people already know. There is nothing new or complicated or surprising here. Everybody knows that a phone call is more effective than email, and yet we email. Everyone knows that referrals are a good way to grow business, and yet we don't ask for them very much.

I start nearly every keynote and workshop by saying: "Everything we're going to talk about today, you already know. And I know you know." Now we are asking them to *do* what they know. That's the thing: knowing what to do to grow sales won't make you any money, and it won't help your customers one bit. To grow sales, we have to do what we know. It's the only way things happen.

They Are All Easy

Over time, and with great intentionality, I have stripped away as much complexity as possible from the Outgrow system of predictable revenue growth. There's nothing complex or difficult in these communications. There's no need to learn a new kind of sale, like consultative selling. There's no need to challenge customers. And there is absolutely no directive to build pain, because there's enough pain in the world. Your company exists to *help* people, not build more pain for them.

Outgrow techniques are super easy and completely common sense. It immediately makes sense to customer-facing people that DYK questions are effective in educating customers about what else they can buy from you. It immediately makes sense that following up on quotes more will close more of them.

They Are Difficult to Resist

The reason these actions are fast, obvious, and easy is because people would resist them if they weren't. If they required a lot of time to do, were complicated, or required learning a new way to sell, your people would simply avoid doing them. Always remember that your staff's ability to resist change is much stronger than your ability to make lasting change. They've had a career's worth of experience in making things go away. They are exceptionally good at it. And it's not their fault, because they've seen most new initiatives come and go.

Outgrow is different. Outgrow *must* be different, or you won't benefit from years of predictable, proactive growth. In fact, I want it to be downright embarrassing for people to resist making these communications. (Imagine saying to a resistant salesperson, "Why exactly are you against telling our customers what else they can buy from us?") Even so, we won't get everybody to come on board. Much more on resistance and how to deal with it in chapter 9.

They Are Helpful

Each of the Outgrow communications is helpful to the recipient. They don't annoy, pester, or pitch. They make salespeople the opposite of what they fear being when they communicate proactively (as discussed in chapter 2). Customers are happy to receive these communications, because it helps them (1) do their jobs, (2) save time, (3) serve *their* customers better, and (4) do more business with you, a trusted partner.

When your team offers additional products and services that your customers aren't buying now, they are helping them buy more in one place, rather than multiple places. Almost all customers want "their person" instead of "their four persons." When you follow up on quotes and proposals, you are reminding the customer to take action about something that's important to them. This is helpful to them. When you ask for referrals, you are helping the customer help their friend or colleague. Every one of these techniques is helpful—and downright valuable—to your customers and prospects.

They Are Never Just to Catch Up

I have a client who is the CEO of a large wholesale distributor, and he often tells his people, "Never just call to catch up; always have a purpose." These communications give your Outgrowers a *reason* to be in touch. With Outgrow, your customers are always receiving value from your people that they simply don't get anywhere else.

They All Help with Customer Retention

In addition to maximizing your sales with current customers and bringing new customers into the fold, these Outgrow communications help you keep the customers you already have. I've started work with clients who had a painful 25% attrition rate. So, even if you add 20% all new business, which is a terrific growth year in most cases, your overall growth would be down 5%.

Why do they go away? Because of silence. Because when you are not in front of them (on the phone or in person), they are not thinking about you. One of my clients calls it "death by a thousand cuts," where competitors come and swipe away a little bit of trust at a time. They take a little bit of your relationship with each communication *they* make while you are quiet. They take a little bit of your revenue, over and over, and you are unlikely to notice unless you're actively running the kinds of "decreasing revenue customers lists" that we talked about in chapter 4. With Outgrow, customers stay with you—and do more business with you—because they see you putting in the effort to try to help them.

They Do Not Require Any Financial Investment

These communications create revenue growth with the people you already have. You don't need to hire anybody, and you don't need to acquire any companies to capture the growth these techniques create. Conversely, the great majority of your competition can *only* grow this way. Hire more salespeople, expand into other territories, or bolt on other companies with business you can absorb into yours. Outgrow is different because it's growth via organic selling. Or, if you wish, growth through effort.

Additionally, there is no advertising to purchase, lists to buy, internet ads to invest in, and no clicks to pay for. In fact, there's *nothing* to pay for. These are behaviors that cost nothing but a few seconds, or a few minutes, of your existing people's time. It's cost-free growth.

They Require Some Confidence and Boldness

Money is not required to implement Outgrow action, but confidence and boldness are. For the great majority of sales and customer service people, most of these communications are uncomfortable.

It's not comfortable to most people to ask about what business they're not getting. It's not comfortable to ask for referrals or about quotes that are outstanding. This is why we build Outgrow on a foundation of confidence and boldness, which originates from the incredibly positive feedback of your happy customers, as I covered in chapter 2.

They Remove Timing as an Obstacle

Outgrow communications take timing off the table. Normally when your people call a customer and offer a new product or service, the odds of them needing that service *at that moment* are pretty low. But when they're consistently showing up, communicating, and offering to help, it doesn't matter if the customers need something at those precise moments. Because when customers do need it, who will they go to? To the people who have been actively trying to help them over time, or those they haven't heard from?

A consistent irony of Outgrow is that the more your people call customers, the more incoming calls they will receive from customers. Even if they are not getting sales in the moment, with these communications, they are earning future business by demonstrating their commitment and interest to their customers. Each communication is a small deposit into an interest-bearing account that pays out intermittently but handsomely! And like a slot machine, *any* communication can lead to a small, *or spectacular*, payout. That's just one reason that Outgrowers find these communications addicting. "I want to do it more," they often tell me. Because the wins can come quickly, and they also come over time. It's a fun and rewarding way to sell!

They All Make You Stand Out from Your Competition

Each of these Outgrow communications helps your company rise above the competition. The reason is simple: *they* are not running Outgrow. Their salespeople are not showing up proactively. They aren't asking what else your customers need and letting them know they would like to help them. With your simple follow-ups and proactive calls, you are doing work that shows your customers you care more about them, and are more interested in doing more business with them, than your competitors.

Frequently, customers tell Outgrowers, "You're the only one calling me like this; the others must not care." This is a powerful and memorable message to hear from your customers. They are telling your people, as a concrete fact, that you're making efforts beyond anything they get from your competition. You are selling more by caring more.

REMEMBER, YOU ARE ASSIGNING THESE ACTIONS TO YOUR OUTGROWERS

A reminder here that the actions on the following pages are meant to be assigned, along with a target quantity of each, on a weekly basis, to your salespeople, customer service people, and any other customer-facing people participating in Outgrow. So, as you review these actions, think about how they will work for your company, and your customers.

A good starting point is about 15 total actions weekly (three per day), with some DYK and rDYK questions included, making it easier for your team to rack up sales-growing communications with customers. Also, it's perfectly reasonable to assign different actions to different roles. For example, you might ask your outside salespeople to make more proactive calls but your customer service people to ask more DYKs and rDYKs because they get many incoming calls each week.

I will take you through this in detail in the next chapter, with multiple examples of assigning actions.

There are two groups of Outgrow communications. The first set of communications are powerful revenue-growing statements to make *during* your proactive calls or in-person conversations. We call these Outgrow Asks. They are the ingredients in the recipe. I lay these out first so we can apply them in the second set of communications, which are the Outgrow Calls.

OUTGROW ASKS

Many of these have come up in the text already, but they are shown together in the following pages, with definitions and examples.. These communications are designed to be spoken to your customers, on the phone or in person. All of them can be used on outbound proactive calls as well as incoming reactive calls with your customers and prospects.

The Did You Know Question (DYK)

Purpose: To inform and educate your customers about additional products and services they can buy from you. Each DYK should be about one product or service that your customers can buy.

Success Rate: 20% of DYK questions close business. We know this from tens of millions of DYKs asked, logged, and tracked over about 20 years of implementation. It's a statistical fact that if your people ask five DYK questions, on average one will turn into a line item over time. Ask 500, and you will add 100 new line items to your business with your customers. So the goal, of course, is to maximize the number of customer-facing people asking DYKs. The more they ask, the more they will sell.

Examples:

- Did you know we have the Carrier furnace line?

- Do you want me to add pipe, tape, filters, and drain line to this? [That's four DYKs in three seconds.]

- Did you know we sell caustic soda?

- How are you on your business insurance?

- Do you need any intellectual property filings?

- What about one-by-fours? [A lumber measurement.]

- Did you know we can sell these in drums or totes? [That's two DYKs.]

Finer Points:

- Each DYK is about one product or service.

- DYKs focus on things customers can pay you for. It's okay to mention things they cannot pay for, such as, *Did you know we have been in business over 100 years?* But these statements need to be accompanied by mentions of products and services the customer can buy. They also don't count for tracking purposes.

- Stack them. Ask multiple DYKs to the same customer.

- If your people ask three DYKs together—for instance, *Did you know I do keynote speeches, workshops, and sales kickoff meetings?*—they should take credit for three DYKs in the tracking form detailed in the next section.

The Reverse Did You Know Question (rDYK)

Purpose: To let the customer name additional products or services that they need but do not currently buy from you.

Success Rate: 80%. Four out of five times, the customer will happily share with you what they buy elsewhere. Again, this statistic is based on millions of rDYKs asked, logged, and tracked by hundreds of clients over over 20 years of Outgrow implementations. Obviously, this is an extraordinarily high success rate. It is, frankly, as close to a sure thing as salespeople can get in their profession. Sometimes the answer will be "We buy everything from you." This may be true, but you may want to confirm by asking some DYKs about products or services you think they could benefit from but do not currently buy from you.

Examples:

- What else do you need to be quoted?

- What else are you buying from my competition that I can help you with?

- We're going to have a delivery to you next week; what else would you like me to add to it? [This is an incredibly effective question for product companies.]

- What else is on your wish list?

- What's going on today? [It's fascinating that customers will often launch into the products and services they need from you when asked this question.]

Finer Points:

- The rDYK is the "what else" question.

- Your people should ask one rDYK question during every single conversation.

- This is actually the single most effective Outgrow communications technique, both in terms of success rate and the sheer quantity of products and services the customer will name.

- The DYK fires products and services at the customer, and you have to hope to hit a bull's eye, one at a time. The rDYK simply asks the customer what else they need, and they tell us—often in bunches of products and services at once.

The Pivot to the Sale (Pivot)

Purpose: To close the business being discussed now.

Success Rate: 25%, which is much higher than *not* asking for the business. One of four requests for the business is rewarded with the customer thanking your people with money!

Examples:

- When would you like us to deliver?

- When do you want to start this project?

- When can I expect the purchase order?

- How would you like to pay?

- How many do you want?

- Do you want to lock this in before next month's price increase?

- I can have this to you by Monday. [Not a question like the others.]

Finer Points:

- This is the "when" question.

- Like the rDYK "what else" question, it should be asked by your Outgrowers during every single conversation. What else do you need? When do you want that?

- Pivot after every DYK.

- The customer has been talking with you about your products or services, and you have had a fairly detailed conversation about their needs. At the end of it, ask to help them with this business. You are not bothering or annoying or selling to them. You are simply asking to make their lives easier. If they don't say "yes, I want it" or "no, I don't," they have to think about it again in the future.

- It's only fair to ask the customer to finally sell them the product or service you've both spent time formulating.

- These pivots to the sale can be used following each DYK and rDYK in conversation.

The Pivot to the Next Conversation (Pivot-C)

Purpose: To schedule the next call or meeting.

Success Rate: 75% schedule the next conversation. Sometimes it's not time to ask for the business yet. Or perhaps you deal with longer sales cycles. If your business opportunity requires another conversation (or a series of them), customers tend to easily and happily schedule it. Three out of four of these conversation requests succeed, statistically. That's a tremendously rewarding way for your people to progress their opportunity toward a quote, proposal, or close.

Examples:

- When would you like to talk again?

- Let's schedule our conversation before we hang up.

- Since we're talking, what's a good day for us to talk again?

- I can be out there next week—what's good for you?

- I think we should meet and spend some time together. How's the week of the 14th?

- What do you want to do next ?

Finer Points:

- Never hang up the phone or leave a meeting without knowing what the next interaction will be and *when* it will happen. If there is nothing scheduled for this opportunity, you will probably lose track of it and not follow up at the correct time. Even in my small business, if it's not on my calendar, it's probably not going to happen—I'm busy, and my clients and prospects are busy. This pivot to the next conversation gets it on the calendar!

- Sometimes the sales cycle is longer and demands multiple conversations over weeks, months, and even years. The Pivot-C technique allows you to schedule them. Always put the next conversation on the calendar before the current one ends.

- Having these scheduled is valuable to both you *and* your customer or prospect. They don't want to drop the ball on an important project you are helping them with. It helps you both remember.

The Percent of Business Question (%Biz)

Purpose: To ask for more business, and in the process learn how much business you have with a particular customer.

Success Rate: In 85% of these you will learn what percent of their business the customer gives. And in 40% you will uncover new opportunities to work on with the customers you ask.

Examples: The %Biz question is a two-part question:

Part One:

- What percent of your business would you guess we have?

- How much of your business do you think we get?

Part Two:

- That's interesting. You're one of my best customers. What are you doing with the other business? Where's it going? I'd love to get a shot at it.

- How do I earn the rest of that business? I'd sure enjoy working with you on that.

Finer Points:

- The customer will almost always answer your question about how much of their business comes to you. So, at minimum, you will learn tremendously valuable information about what you have and what is available with them.

- You will also learn what's happening with the work you're not getting. You will know where it goes, and why. Is it because of price? Availability? Or maybe they're just one of these companies that is required to spread their eggs across various baskets. This happens. But you probably don't know if this is the case today, and you will after asking the %Biz question.

- About 40% of the customers you ask this question to will tell you the specific products and services they purchase elsewhere, and in many cases they will give you a shot at it.

- Most Outgrowers do not start with this question. I think the reason is that it's a little more complex than the others (involving two steps) and also it's probably a bit more threatening than the others. It requires more confidence and boldness.

- If you'd like your people to implement this communication, it will be important to actively assign it in your weekly target actions. People tend not to get to it on their own, as they do with DYKs and rDYKs.

The Internal Referral Request (iREF)

Purpose: To be connected to additional potential buyers at a current customer company.

Success Rate: 66%. Quite high, right? So why not ask?

Examples:

- Who else do you work with who I should be helping?

- What other people do similar work to yours who I can be helping?

- Who else do I need to know at your firm?

- What other locations / divisions / regions / buildings / profit centers are there that I should be trying to help the way that I help you? Who should I be talking with there?

Finer Points:

- As discussed in the previous chapter, salespeople are often not selling to every person who buys what they sell at a company.

- People love to give referrals, especially internally within their company. They help a colleague, and you. The colleague is happy, and you've been rewarded with more business. Also, when they need something from you in the future, you will be more inclined to help them above others.

- Note that none of the questions here are yes or no questions. They are all *who else* and *what else* questions. As a general rule, try to stay away from yes or no questions in sales situations, and especially so with referral requests. It's easy to do, and *most* salespeople ask: "Do you know anyone else I should be working with?" What's the easy, obvious answer for the customer? "No, I don't think so!"

- This is low-hanging fruit. You're already doing good business with the customer, and your trust together is strong. You are in their system as a provider, and they are in your system as a customer. It's easy to help this company more.

- If the company is a contractor or a law firm or an interior design agency, and you are doing business with one of their people but there are 5 to 10 other people in the company, you are likely to *easily* grow your business exponentially with this company. And why not? All those people not getting your value today are suffering through your competition.

- This is another reason why it's important to think of your customers in terms of the people you are helping rather than as the companies they work for. When you think of corporations, it closes off considering additional potential buyers.

The External Referral Request (xREF)

Purpose: To be connected to prospective customers who your current customer knows.

Success Rate: 66% if you follow these three steps.

Three-Step Examples: Who, How, When

1. **Who** else do you know, like yourself, who I can help the way that I help you? [Then be silent while the person thinks. They're not quiet because they are uncomfortable. They are quiet because they're thinking.]

2. Thank you. I appreciate this. **How** should I reach out? Do you prefer that I contact them and use your name, or would you like to connect us? [Most people will choose to make the connection, often over email.]

3. I know how busy you are. So that I don't bother you, **when** do you think you might get to it? [They will say something like, "I'll call or email you both by the end of the week," or "I'll send you their contact info by the end of this week."] Okay, great. So if I don't hear from you by end of day Friday, is it okay with you if I follow up with you on this on Monday? [I've never had a client tell me no.]

Finer Points:

-   As mentioned, silence is everything here. Ask your question and look away and count to 100 if you have to. Sing a song in your head (not out loud). But do not speak until your customer gives you an answer.

- Like internal referrals, people love giving external referrals. They have a friend in the industry who you can help. They know you are great to work with. They connect you two. Who comes out best in this exchange? Always, the referrer. They get to help their friend and send you business. And, again, if they need something urgently tomorrow, you will be more inclined to drop what you are doing to help them because they just sent you a referral. You will feel like you owe them this. And that's another reason people love to give referrals.

- After the customer responds to your **when** request, write down the date. Also, be sure to write down the day you said you will follow up. And absolutely put it on your calendar with an alert. You committed to following up— you should do everything you can to do so. It would be professional malpractice to get a referral and not follow up on the connection or contact information.

Communicating a Testimonial (Comm)

Purpose: To demonstrate to a prospective customer how happy your current customers are, and help make them aspire to—and desire—the same value. Here, you are sharing the testimonials from your customers that you collected in the qualitative interviews described in chapter 2. This communication can be done by phone or text message.

Example:

- We have a customer similar to you, and here is what they have to say about us. Quote [then read into the phone or paste into the text message the testimonial you have selected], close quote. I'd love the opportunity to help you this way. When can we connect to discuss what that looks like? [This is a Pivot-C, to the next conversation.]

Finer Points:

- These are most often delivered to prospects, not customers.

- You can also target current customers who you would like to expand business with by sharing a testimonial from a different customer who is buying the products or services you wish to sell to the recipient of this testimonial.

- You are either speaking this to the customer on a proactive call or you are texting it. Like everything else in this chapter, this is not an email.

- If *you* said to the prospect that you will save them time, and that you will have a great, friendly relationship revolving around mutual trust and respect, it would be kind of weird. And awkward. But when you put quotes around it and lead with "our customers say . . ." and end with "we'd like to do this for you," it's just the truth. It's credible. And the prospect is not only listening intently, they are likely desiring the same benefits your other customers are praising.

OUTGROW CALLS

Proactive phone calls are the core of the Outgrow system for revenue growth. They are caring, relationship-building communications with customers and prospects when nothing is wrong. This section introduces a simple, three-part structure for all of the proactive calls detailed here.

The Outgrow Call Structure: Three Parts, Three Minutes

Here is a general structure for all of our Outgrow proactive calls. We'll start with this base three-part approach and make small modifications for the specific applications covered further in this chapter. This approach often takes just three minutes.

Outgrow Proactive Call Structure	
Three Parts	**Language**
The Opening	I was thinking about you. How is your family?
Shift to the Business	DYKs and rDYKs: • What are you working on that I can help you with? • What are you doing with my competition that I can help with? • Wanted to let you know we recently got products X and Y in. • I was working on service X and Y with another client, and thought that would work really well for you. • What else is going on? What do you need?
Pivot	• When would you like us to do/deliver this? • When can I expect the PO? • Want me to just add it to the current PO? • I can come see you next week, and we can nail this down.

Part One: The Opening

Because Outgrow is so complex, we call part one of Outgrow Calls the opening (that's a joke!). This is where you spend a moment catching up with your customer. It might include lines like:

- I was thinking about you because . . .

- How's your family?

- What are the kids doing? (If it has been a while, you might say, "How old are the kids now?")

- How was your trip?

This first part of the conversation is brief, and you're asking the kinds of questions you'd ask of a friend. The reason for this is the more a customer can think of you as a friend, the more easily they will do more business with you.

Part Two: Shift to the Business

Now we move the conversation toward business. This part includes your DYK and rDYK questions. It's best to stack them, and use multiple questions in your conversation. It looks like this:

- So what do you have going on there this week/month/quarter? (rDYK)

- What else do you need me to put together for you? (rDYK)

- Hey, I'm going to have that delivery out to you this week—what else do you want me add to it? (rDYK)

- I got some product X, Y, and Z—how many do you want me to send? (DYK)
    - I can have product y to you next week—does that work? (Pivot)

- Did you know we have product A, B, and C as of last week? (DYK)

- How are your machines working? What else do you need help with? (rDYK)

- What else do you need quoted? (rDYK)
  - Should I go ahead and add that to the order? (Pivot)

This is probably more questions than you would ask in this part, but I wanted to give you a sense of the options. You might just need one or two of these, or you can keep probing in different ways until you find something they need that you can provide.

You can see there is room to pivot to the sale after the DYKs and rDYKs in this section, individually for each product or service discussed. Then we go on to the large, overall pivot.

Part Three: Pivot to the Sale or the Next Commitment

The final part of the conversation is your pivot to the sale or the next conversation, depending on which one is appropriate.

Pivots to the sale include:

- When would you like us to ship this?

- When can we expect the PO?

- When do you start work?

Pivots to the next conversation can be:

- When do you want me to follow up with you on this?

- I can be in your area in a couple of weeks—what's a good day for you?

- Let's look at our calendars while we're on the phone and set a day to speak next.

Asking for the business or the next commitment is not pushy or used car salesperson–like. It shows your customers that you are interested in helping them. In fact, you *are* helping them, because if they accept your offer to buy or talk again, this is not something they have to think about again. And that is very valuable to your customers.

ON EVERY CALL: WHAT ELSE, AND WHEN?

Here's an easy rule of thumb for your people: on *every* interaction with a customer, they should be asking *what else* (that's an rDYK) and *when* (that's a pivot). This means during:

- Proactive calls from Outgrowers to customers

- In-person meetings and visits

- Incoming calls and inquiries

How would this work when customers call your people? They would address the issue the customer is calling about. That's the customer service work they excel at, all day long. Then, when the issue has been dealt with—or, at least, a plan has been made to do so—the Outgrower can shift to the rDYK:

Anything else on that item or issue? No? Great, listen, while we're talking, what else do you have coming up next week (or month) that I can get going here for you?

Ask the question and stay silent while they think, and don't talk until they answer the question.

After the customer answers: *When would you like us to start on this? or Will you send the PO today?* or, if it's not time for that yet, *How's next Tuesday or Wednesday to finalize this?*

Emphasize that your team always ask *what else.*

And after that, they should always ask *when.*

This way, every interaction turns into a Wallet Share Expansion opportunity to help your customers more.

ALWAYS LEAVE A VOICEMAIL

One of the most frequent questions salespeople ask me is, "Should I leave a voicemail?"

My answer is always, "Unequivocally, yes."

If they don't leave a message, how does the customer know they tried to connect and made an effort to help? Without a voicemail, the customer doesn't get to hear your salesperson's name. Or your company's name. Even if the customer doesn't return the call, there is great value in the customer hearing your salesperson's name and their voice. It's a reminder that they should go to you when a need arises.

So why do salespeople avoid leaving a message? They usually say it's because "I don't want to look desperate," which is a part of the painful and damaging default mindset. Our job—yours and mine—is to help them understand that if they called and did not leave a message it is as if they didn't call at all. That call is like the tree falling in the forest. If the phone number isn't recognized, the customer has no idea your salesperson called. If the phone number *is* recognized, it's even worse: now the customer is wondering why your person called and didn't leave a message. Perhaps it *was* a spam call. There is nothing to tell them otherwise.

Here Is Your General Voicemail Script

Tom, it's Alex Goldfayn. I was thinking about you because I have a client [or customer] similar to you, and they're doing [or buying] some really interesting things that I think would also work well for you. I'd like to tell you about that, and of course I'd love to catch up as well and hear your latest. Here's my number; please call when you have a moment.

Why is the message like this? Here are some details on this intentional structure:

- It's very short. At my speaking pace, this is a 12-second message. I timed it. If you speak slowly, it's probably an 18-second message.

- If it must be transcribed, the text is readable in moments.

- "I was thinking about you" tells the customer they are important to you.

- Mentioning a similar customer "buying some interesting things" that you feel would also work for this person is very compelling. It shows you have really put some thought and preparation into this phone call.

- It's also interesting to find out what their peers—and, presumably, their competition—are doing with you. You are offering valuable market intelligence. Also, if the competition is buying these things from you, perhaps this customer will feel like they should too.

- With this structure, your people are respectfully offering customers *and* prospects—it works equally well for both—value.

AFTER YOU LEAVE A VOICEMAIL, SEND A TEXT MESSAGE

Immediately after leaving your message, send a text message:

Per my voicemail, how is Tuesday or Wednesday to speak?

Here is why:

- Statistically, we know that two-thirds of the people you leave a voicemail for, followed by a text message, will respond back to your salespeople. This is based on tens of millions of proactive calls logged, tracked, and analyzed.

- We also know that two-thirds of the customers who get back to you will do so via text message.

- Which means that without sending the text, your call return rate goes from 67% to 22%. That's a dramatic impact.

- A voicemail followed by a text turns the customer's decision into a choice of *how to get back to you*, instead of a yes or no decision about calling you back. This is where we want to be.

- The text message acts to turn your salespeople's proactive outreach into a planned, or scheduled, call. This will force your customers to think about and prepare for the conversation, and what we find in the Outgrow process is that they come prepared to discuss your products and services.

HOW LONG DOES IT TAKE TO MAKE THESE CALLS?

Because these are proactive phone calls, your salespeople will frequently be leaving voicemails, followed by text messages. This will be the most common outcome. As a result, they will often complete their three calls in less than five minutes. This is one of the most helpful parts of Outgrow: it can be implemented very quickly, often in just moments, each day. Because if it took a long time, your busy salespeople would simply use that as a reason to resist.

I run my business on three proactive phone calls a day. Removing 10 business days for holidays and off days, that's 750 calls in a year. As detailed just above, statistically, two-thirds of the recipients, all of whom can buy something from me, or advance my business forward—500 of them—will return my communication. I simply don't need any more than that. (However, when things slow down, I increase the calls to five daily.)

If I'm in meetings or delivering a speech or workshop, I still make my calls before my session begins. If the recipient happens to surprisingly answer, I tell them, "Tom, it's Alex Goldfayn. Listen, I've got a workshop today, but I was thinking about you recently and wanted to hear your latest and tell you a bit about what's happening here, which I think might be useful to you. Can we schedule some time on our calendars for next week?" This will add an appointment phone call to your calendar.

So, even when they do pick up, the call can take five minutes or less. But if I *have* the time, I am happy to talk to them for a few minutes and have a pleasant, friendly, feel-good conversation with somebody I can potentially help. They appreciate it, and we both enjoy it.

WHEN TO MAKE YOUR CALLS

Mark Twain said if you have to eat a frog, do it first thing in the morning because it won't taste any better later in the day. Making proactive calls is something most people are uncomfortable doing, so the best approach is to tackle this challenge first thing in the morning, when you have the most focus and energy. (This morning focus and energy is often totally wasted by many people on emails and internet browsing.) I do my calls before 9 AM each day, and then I feel good the rest of the day. I've done the most difficult thing—I've exercised my revenue growth muscles.

Mark Twain also said if you have to eat *two* frogs, eat the biggest one first. That is, make the most difficult call first. Get it out of the way and move on.

THE FIRST CALL IS THE HARDEST

Because proactive calls are avoided and procrastinated on, the first one is the most difficult to make. That's because we need to overcome all the resistance, entrenched and imposing as it is. You'll find the second and third ones much easier to make, and it might even start to feel good to you, and you may not want to stop at three calls. If you're feeling momentum, put it to use and keep going.

Because the wins come quickly on these proactive calls, Outgrowers find making them addicting. That's because the research and foundations of behavioral psychology tell us the reinforcement that creates the greatest effort is intermittent and positive. That is, when we make calls, we get positive outcomes frequently, but irregularly. We don't know when they will come. They feel great when they do occur—a nice conversation, an exchange of pleasantries, a "nice to hear from you," a new opportunity uncovered, a meeting scheduled, or a quote requested. And so, we chase the way those rewards make us feel. We start to appreciate and enjoy the work that predictably grows sales because it frequently makes us feel good!

Proactive Calls to Customers on Your Lists

The customers and prospects here are described in detail in chapter 4, so for each group of customers and prospects here I will give only a brief definition of the group and a sample script your salespeople can use. Scripts follow the Outgrow three-part, three-minute proactive call structure outlined in the previous sections.

Calls to Zero Dark 30 Customers

These are customers who have done a significant amount of business with you over the last year (pick your number) but zero over the last month.

Part One: The Opening

- *Hi, Sally, it's Tom Jones. I was thinking about you because I noticed we haven't done as much business together over the last month, and I wanted to check in. How are you? How's your family?*

Part Two: Shift to the Business

- **DYK:** *You had been buying 10 units of product X most months, but I don't think you've ordered any recently.*

  - **Intermediate Pivot:** *Do you want me to get some out to you?*

  - **Another DYK:** *What about products Y and Z? How are you on those? [Two products are mentioned, so your salesperson would take credit for two DYKs.]*

    - **Another Intermediate Pivot:** *Should we add those to the order as well?*

  - **rDYK:** *What else do you need?*

Part Three: Pivot to the Sale

- **Pivot:** *I'll get the quote together and have it to you. When can I expect the PO?*

- **Another Pivot:** *Great, if I don't hear from you by that day, is it okay to reach out to you about this?*

In this interaction, your salesperson would log and take credit for a proactive call, three DYKs, one rDYK, and four pivots to the sale, for a total of eight total Outgrow actions—in a conversation that probably took three minutes.

Calls to Customers on Revenue Autopilot

These are customers who are buying a consistent set of products and services, accounting for a narrow band of total monthly revenue. Their purchasing is on autopilot because they have niched you for the specific things they buy.

Part One: The Opening

- *Hi, Mark, it's Christy Owens. I know it has been a while since we talked, but I wanted to pick up the phone and catch up. You guys are an important customer for me, and I wanted to see how else I can help. But before we go there, how is your family? What are the kids doing?*

Part Two: Shift to the Business

- ***rDYK:*** *So what's going on with your business? [This is a legitimate and effective rDYK.]*

- ***DYK:*** *Did you know we carry products a and b now? [Two DYKs]*

- ***Intermediate Pivot:*** *Can I add those to your next order?*

- ***rDYK:*** *What else do you have coming up that we can help you with?*

- ***rDYK:*** *What projects are coming up?*

Part Three: Pivot to the Sale or Next Conversation

- ***Pivot-C:*** *Would love to get our business back to where we were and, ideally, even beyond that. Our work is important to me. When would you like to get together to solidify this? [This is a pivot to the next conversation.]*

This brief conversation would be logged as one proactive call, two DYKs, three rDYKs, and two pivots for a total of eight proactive actions.

Calls to Customers with Decreasing Revenue

These are customers whose revenue is on the decline. They are buying less and less.

Part One: The Opening

- *Hi, Cindy, it's Mark Ellis. How are you? How's your family? How was summer for the kids? I was thinking about you because a customer of mine is doing some interesting things with us that I think would work well for you too. I took a look at your account, and I noticed that we're not sending you as much products X and Y like we used to.*

  [This is more of a customer service outreach, where you are asking if something happened, or if something is wrong. It gives the customer a chance to vent, which is always better than stewing in silence about something that upsets them. You might learn nothing negative occurred and you had some business poached by competition.]

Part Two: Shift to the Business

- **rDYK:** *How are you doing with your inventory of products X and Y?*

- **Intermediate Pivot:** *I'd love to have the opportunity to earn that business back.*

- **rDYK:** *What else is happening that I can help you with?*

- **%Biz:** *What percent of your business would you guess we have?*

- **DYK:** *Are you all sourcing services X and Y these days? [Two DYKs]*

Part Three: Pivot to the Sale or Next Conversation

- **Pivot-C:** *Why don't we get together in the next couple of weeks and cement all this? I can be there in two weeks on Tuesday or Wednesday. Is one of those better than the other?*

This conversation will be logged as one proactive call, two DYKs, two rDYKs, one %Biz, and two pivots for eight total proactive actions.

Calls to Customers Who Used to Buy but Stopped

This group of customers are past customers with whom you no longer do business. This call is your attempt to get that customer back. It doesn't have to be everything you once did together. We're just trying to get them to dip a toe back in the water.

Part One: The Opening

- *Hi, Chris, it's Kathy calling. Gosh, I didn't realize how long it has been since we talked until I happened to see that we haven't seen any orders from you in over a year. How are you doing? What's new with your family? Everyone doing well? Well, listen, I know we had some problems with inventory back then, but we've made a bunch of fixes—systems and people—and things are much smoother now.*

Part Two: Shift to the Business

- ***Pivot:*** *We'd sure love to get some of your business back. [Then be silent.]*

- ***Pivot:*** *I'd love to earn your business again. [Silence.]*

- ***Pivot:*** *Would you be open to giving us another chance? I'll oversee your account personally. [Silencio!]*

- ***rDYK:*** *Also, I was wondering, what else do you have coming up that we can help with?*

Part Three: Pivot to the Sale or Next Conversation

- ***Pivot:*** *Thank you so much for that. I'm grateful for the opportunity to work with you again. I'll put this first order together, send you a quote, and get it out on Friday if all that works for you. [Pivots can be statements and don't have to be questions.]*

This conversation was a proactive call, four pivots, and an rDYK. Six total swings to be logged.

Calls to Customers with an Outstanding Quote or Proposal

These are quote and proposal follow-up calls. This is the fastest-acting Outgrow call because it generates the most sales dollars the fastest.

Part One: The Opening

- *Hi, Robyn, it's Joe. How are you? All good today? [The opening is quicker here because it's likely you recently spoke at length to put the quote or proposal together.]*

Part Two: Shift to the Business

- *QFU (Quote Follow-Up): Listen, where are you at on that quote? I was thinking about you, and would love to help with that.*

- *rDYK: Great. Anything else you'd like me to add to the quote?*

- *rDYK: What do you have coming up in the next few weeks that you want me to look up for you?*

Part Three: Pivot to the Sale or Next Conversation

- *Pivot: Excellent, so I'll process the order and you'll get the PO to me this morning.*

This is a quick one. A proactive call, a QFU, two rDYKs, and a pivot. Five swings to enter into the tracking form.

Calls to Customers Who Have a Pre-Quote or Proposal Opportunity

These customers are not quite to the quote or proposal stage yet, and the purpose of the call is to move them toward that quote or proposal. You are advancing the business toward the next crucial step.

Part One: The Opening

- *Hey, Cindy, it's Dawn. How are you? Are you guys doing okay in that crazy weather? I was thinking about our last conversation, which I really enjoyed, and I wanted to call . . .*

Part Two: Shift to the Business

- **Pivot:** *. . . to see if you were ready for a proposal on that work we discussed.*

- **Pivot:** *I'd sure like to help you with that project we discussed. [Silence.]*

- **rDYK:** *Is there anything you would like to add to the work, while we're talking about it?*

- **DYK:** *I have several other clients who are working on X and Y with me, actually. [Two DYKs]*

- **Pivot:** *Would you like me to write that up and add it to the proposal?*

Part Three: Pivot to the Sale or Next Conversation

- **Pivot:** *Excellent. I'll put that together and have it to you within 24 hours. [Silence—wait for acknowledgment or okay.]*

- **Pivot:** *And when do you think you'll have it back to me? [Count to 100 in your head, but don't talk.]*

- **Pivot:** *Great, and if I don't hear from you next week, is it okay to follow up the following week?* [Not a word!]

This is a proactive call with six pivots, two DYKs, and one rDYK, for a total of ten actions—in a conversation that is likely less than five minutes.

Calls to Your Large Customers Who Can Buy Even More

These customers, added together, make up the bulk of your revenue, but these calls go to those of them that can buy even more.

Part One: The Opening

- *How are you, Joe? It's Greg calling. Everything going well today?* [This opening can be shorter because I am presuming you speak to these customers frequently.]

Part Two: Shift to the Business

- **rDYK:** *Listen, I know we do a lot of work together, but I was wondering— what else do you have going on that I'm not helping you with?*

- **rDYK:** *What am I not quoting?*

- **Internal Ref:** *Who else do you work with who buys what you buy?*

- **DYK:** *How are you on products X or Y?* [Two DYKs]

Part Three: Pivot to the Sale or Next Conversation

- **Pivot:** *So you think you'll give me that list of products by tomorrow?*

- **Pivot:** *And if I don't hear from you, is it okay to follow up the following day?*

- **Pivot:** *Also, thank you for the referral to your colleague. I'll look for their contact info from you today.*

This is a proactive call, with two rDYKs, two DYKs, one internal referral request, and three pivots to the sale. That's nine total swings of the bat to log.

Calls to Small and Medium Customers Who Can Buy More

This is customer enlargement work, turning smaller customers into bigger customers. These calls go to customers who don't hear from your team very much because of the less significant revenue they drive in your business.

Part One: The Opening

- *Hi, Kristen, it's Alex Goldfayn calling. How are you? How's your family? I know it has been a while since we talked, but I was thinking about you because we just got some product in that I think would be helpful for you.*

Part Two: Shift to the Business

- **DYK:** *We got in products X, Y, and Z, and I know you use those with customers.*

- **Pivot:** *Would you like me to set some aside for you?*

- **rDYK:** *What else do you have coming up that I can help with?*

- **rDYK:** *Is there anything you would like me to add to the truck?*

Part Three: Pivot to the Sale or Next Conversation

- **Pivot:** *Okay, great. I have it written down and will get the quote out to you today, okay?*

- **Pivot:** *When can I expect the purchase order?*

This is a proactive call, with one DYK, two rDYKs, and three pivots, for a total of seven Outgrow actions on this one interaction.

Calls to Prospective Customers

The following two calls are to prospective customers—those you know, and those you do not.

Calls to Prospects You've Talked To Who Did Not Buy

These are prospective customers who went down the road toward a sale with you but ultimately did not buy. They are an extremely valuable and overlooked group of prospects to call on.

Part One: The Opening

- *Hi, Samantha, it's Sabrina Smith calling with XYZ company. How are you? I know we haven't talked in some time, but I was thinking about you and the project [or initial order] we had framed out because I recently had a customer start buying something similar. I really enjoyed our conversations and wanted to check in with you and see if it might make sense to revisit our discussion.*

Part Two: Shift to the Business

- *rDYK: What's going on these days?*

- *rDYK: What are you working on over the next few months?*

- *rDYK: Anything specific come to mind where I can help?*

- *DYK: It's interesting—that other customer that reminded me of you put together a program around A, B, and C.*

- *Pivot:* Is that something we should add to our project?

Part Three: Pivot to the Next Conversation

- *Pivot:* Why don't we get together and edit the proposal together? We can do it on Zoom or in person. What's better for you?

- *Pivot:* How about Friday?

This is a proactive call, with three rDYKs, one DYK, and three pivots, for a total of eight Outgrow actions.

Cold Calls: Calls to Prospects You Have Not Talked To (Cold Calls)

These are calls to customers you are aware of but who are not buying from your company currently. But you know they buy the products or services you sell, and probably do so from your competition. These are cold calls, warmed up as much as possible by anchoring the prospect to the names of your customers and products and services that they recognize.

Part One: The Opening

- *Hello, Tom, it's Chris Smith from ABC Inc. How are you, sir? Listen, I know you are with X Co. now, but I've heard about your work and you have an excellent reputation in our industry. We supply similar products as X Co. to customers like DEF Co. and GHI LLC, which you may know—they're in your area.*

Part Two: Shift to the Business

- *Pivot:* Anyway, I'd love to learn what you're working on and see if I might be able to earn some of your business.

- **rDYK:** *So tell me about your work and the kind of products you need.*

- **DYK:** *Do you use products X, Y, or Z? [Three DYKs]*

- **rDYK:** *What kinds of jobs do you have coming up in the next few months?*

- **DYK:** *Oh, did you know we supply the XYZ line?*

- **rDYK:** *What else would you like me to quote?*

Part Three: Pivot to the Sale or Next Conversation

- **Pivot:** *This all sounds great; let me write it up and send you the quote.*

- **Pivot:** *I'll also send you a credit application—when can I expect that back?*

This five-minute conversation is a proactive call, with three pivots, three rDYKs, and four DYKs. Eleven total Outgrow swings of the bat to log!

Other Proactive Calls Based on Customer Business

Now we move away from proactive calls based on pipeline position to calls based on the business a customer does with you.

Calls to Customers Who Just Got a Product or Service from You

These are calls to people who just received a product or service from your company. These kinds of communications used to be quite common. The last bastion of these communications were car dealerships. The first few cars I purchased in my life, I got a post-delivery call *every* time. Not so over the last decade or so, and as I get older, I've been buying nicer cars. You'd think salespeople would want to lock in the relationship and take simple steps to help ensure a customer returns. They may *want* to, but I wouldn't know it.

These are fantastic activities for customer service people or inside salespeople because they are proactive customer service inquiries first and foremost. Then, once you confirm that all is well with your delivery or service, shift to your rDYKs and DYKs.

Part One: The Opening

- *Hi, Emily, this is Paul calling. How are you? All good in your world? Kiddos doing well? Hey, I'm just calling to make sure everything arrived okay. Everything look good? Do you need anything else on that order?*

- *If you fixed something recently . . .*
  - *Is everything working okay? Nothing causing you problems?*

- *If you provided business services . . .*
  - *How is everything going with what we talked about in our planning session? Any questions? Need anything else from me on that?*

Part Two: Shift to the Business

- *Great!*

- **DYK:** *Listen, I don't know if you knew this, but we also have one-on-one coaching services for the folks that were involved in our session.*

- **rDYK:** *What else do you have coming up that I can help you with?*

- **rDYK:** *Are you thinking about any new hires that I should put on my calendar to be on standby to help with?*

Part Three: Pivot to the Sale or Next Conversation

- **Pivot:** *Listen, it has been great catching up. I'll put it on my calendar to call again two weeks from today—that's Monday the seventh. Good for you?*

This conversation is a proactive call, with one DYK, two rDYKs, and a pivot—five total actions to be logged.

Order History Call

These calls are to customers whose frequency of ordering certain products or services has dropped off. These customers used to buy weekly or monthly, but now it has been several months since they've made a purchase. If they used to buy frequently, but now they've stopped, they haven't stopped buying altogether; they've simply stopped buying from you. So this call is your company's attempt to get the business back. Your people are showing these customers that they (1) noticed, (2) are interested, and (3) are trying to help.

Part One: The Opening

- *Hello, Michelle, it's Bob calling from ABC company. How are you? Did your family trip go well? Listen, we were just talking about you here because we noticed that it has been seven months since you purchased any control panels. You used to buy them twice a month or so.*

Part Two: Shift to the Business

- **Pivot:** *We'd sure like to help you with that again.*

- **DYK:** *We also carry brands X, Y, and Z now, in case you were looking for some different lines. [Three DYKs]*

- **rDYK:** *What else do you have happening over there that I can help with?*

Part Three: Pivot to the Sale or Next Conversation

- **Pivot:** *Okay, great, so I'll write it up and get this out to you. When do you want us to deliver?*

This would be logged as one proactive call, three DYKs, one rDYK, and two pivots, for seven total swings.

No List Required: Calls to Customers Who Email

This category doesn't require a list because every customer-facing person at your company already has a living, breathing, auto-updating, current-to-the-minute list of *these* customers and prospects. This list lives in each person's email inbox. All day long, your people receive emailed requests for products, services, pricing, and customer service issues.

This proactive calling technique turns this incoming flood of items to respond to into an easy list of people to call proactively. These calls go something like this:

Part One: The Opening

- *Hi, Max, it's Alex. I received your email, and I'm putting the quote together for this now.*

  Or . . .

- *Hi, Max, it's Alex. I got your email, and I am checking on that for you right now. I'll let you know as soon I hear . . . But listen, it has been a while since we talked. How are you? How is your family doing?*

Part Two: Shift to the Business

- **rDYK:** *What else do you have going on that I can help you with?*

- **rDYK:** What am I not quoting you?

- **DYK:** We've had some new product lines come in since we last talked, including A, B, C, and D. [This is four DYKs.]

Part Three: Pivot to the Sale or Next Conversation

- **Pivot:** Would you like me to add any of those items to this quote?

- **Pivot-C:** Should we get together to talk about that?

Your Outgrower would take credit for one proactive call, four DYKs, two rDYKs, and two pivots for a total of nine actions.

One More Communication: The Handwritten Note

What's even rarer than a proactive call? The basically extinct handwritten note.

The proactive calls put you in very rare air—among approximately 5% of companies and people who sell. The handwritten note, on the other hand, makes you basically singular. If you send a customer a handwritten note, it is likely to be the only one they receive this year.

Sure, they might get a greeting card for their birthday, or printed and mail-merged holiday cards, but a handwritten note is different. Outgrow notes are not thank-you notes. Rather, they are human notes that include a line or two about something you recently talked about with your customer. This can include something they did on vacation, a sports team you discussed, a home improvement project, or dropping the kids off at school. It's okay to say thank you in these notes, but it should be secondary to something that was recently discussed. Here is an example:

Dear Tom,

Really enjoyed our conversation this week, and I hope you had a wonderful, relaxing break in Florida. Can't wait to hear about it!

Warm regards,
Alex Goldfayn

Or . . .

Dear Tom,

I'm sorry your Rams lost to my Bears this week—it was an exciting game. Your Rams sure look to be in great shape for the future!

See you soon,
Alex Goldfayn

Please note there is no mention of business. Or your upcoming call or meeting. There is not even a phone number included, although you can *handwrite* it under your name if you'd like. Absolutely no business cards should be placed in these envelopes. You will find that nearly everyone you send a note like this to will get back to you. Most of these follow-up communications will come by email, which is ironic, but ultimately, good for future business expansion.

CASE STUDY: LEADING INDICATORS OF REVENUE GROWTH

For over 100 years, UCC Environmental has been developing highly engineered material handling systems and pollution control systems for the power generation industry, mining, and other categories. Their large installations are built uniquely to each customer's specific situation and are used to clean wastewater ponds of ash and chemicals. I share these details with you because their sales cycles are very long. These are highly complex sales involving many different stakeholders because they are engineering, building, installing, and maintaining highly complicated machinery.

Most of this custom install work is long-term proposal based. And so we track proposals sent against Outgrow actions. This metric is a powerful leading indicator of their future sales growth. It looks like this:

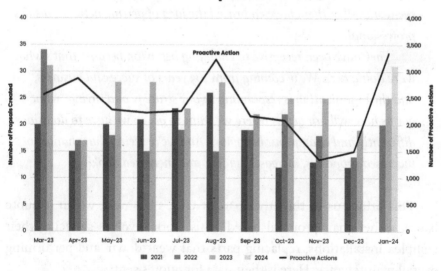

Number of Proposals Created

UCC launched Outgrow in March 2023, so it's the first month tracked. The graph above tracks proposals sent year over year with the bars. The line graph tracks the Outgrow selling actions. As you can see, it took two months of Outgrow proactivity (in March and April) to impact proposal count. Then, as long as actions were up, proposals stayed up. But in September, actions fell, and so did proposals. And in December you see the impact of several months of lower proactivity.

At this point, leadership strongly and repeatedly communicated to its 72 Outgrowers that action counts were going in the wrong direction and wouldn't sustain the desired growth. And, indeed, the action counts and ensuing proposal volume in January 2024 show that the message resonated. Outgrow actions and proposals shot up.

I asked Kevin McDonough, executive vice president and chief revenue officer at UCC and sitting in the seat of top Outgrow executive there, for his take on the impact Outgrow has had on his sales organization. Here is his answer:

> *The first impact is genuine enthusiasm. Change is hard. I expected resistance to Outgrow. I have been pleasantly surprised with the opposite: with a genuine enthusiasm for the process, the discipline, and the work. All of them have embraced the idea of getting better as a sales professional.*
>
> *They have been receptive to changing behavior, because that's what we're doing here. We're coming from 103 years of successful business, and the organization is responding to our strategy and saying "what got us here will not get us where we want to go, so we have to do things differently and change our behavior." And we're seeing that change in increased proposals, increased quotes, and increased bookings.*

This brings us to the other part of UCC's business, which is quote based, rather than proposal based. This work involves servicing their complex installations, replacing parts that wear down, and performing overall maintenance. Here is their data for quotes sent:

Number of Parts Quotes Generated

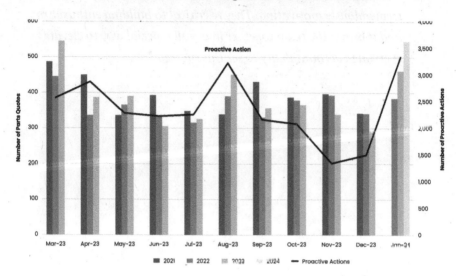

Here, the quotes follow Outgrow actions precisely—actions up, quotes up; actions down, quotes down. So the counts of behavior-based Outgrow actions is a near-perfect, immediate indicator of sales success.

What are the keys to the success of UCC's Outgrow implementation? Kevin answered in list form:

1. *"The first area is our leadership team has bought in. We speak the same language, and we are aligned as a leadership team on what the Outgrow purpose is."*

2. *"The second key is regular check-in, the Monday Huddles, the Monthly Reviews—our quarterly meetings with our Outgrow Advisor are absolutely essential to our engagement with our Outgrowers.*

3. *"The third is the data. The data ensures our people are participating. The data is also inspirational. If you look at the actions leaderboard, the top third or so—man, they want to be at the top of that leaderboard. It's important to them! So I think when you have that visibility of the data, it's a motivating force for people to want more.*

4. *"Last area: success stories. Those are absolutely critical and tremendously motivating. They're critical to building enthusiasm and it brings the team together in a really special way to elevate everyone's accountability to see this succeed."*

Chapter 7
THE WEEKLY PROCESS

The Outgrow process you will run is a feedback loop with five key parts for revenue growth. Using the communications detailed in the last chapter, you or your Outgrow leader will (1) assign a quantity of target actions for your customer-facing teams to do this week. As your team (2) makes these communications to customers and prospects throughout the week, they will (3) log them into a tech-based tracking system. This is where you will track their swings and the opportunities they uncover. From here, the system will give you (4) data and analytics that will be shared with all participants, and, if you wish, company-wide. Finally, using the same system, you will collect and (5) communicate the wins, or success stories, they share. This will formally and publicly recognize the good work that participants are doing and will teach the group what is working, *motivating* them to do more. This is a week in the life of an Outgrow organization.

The rest of this chapter will lay out each component, but first let's discuss your options for a technology system you can use to run Outgrow.

TECHNOLOGY FOR LOGGING AND TRACKING

In the beginning, the early versions of the Outgrow process ran on pieces of paper. Customer-facing people would log their proactive communications on paper trackers and submit them to an administrative person like an office manager, who would enter each person's actions into a spreadsheet. From there, we moved to direct entry into Microsoft Excel (Google Sheets was not yet in existence). Today, we use one of two options: your existing CRM or the Outgrow Tracking System (OTS) provided to you in one of the Outgrow offerings. Both will be described here.

But first, while Outgrow requires a technology-enabled home base, the exact system doesn't matter. All that matters is that there is a system. You need a place for people to capture the actions they implement and track their opportunities so that they can follow up on them. Additionally, the leader, managers, and the Outgrowers need the data that is generated by Outgrow. The data is critical because it is a totally accurate predictor of what your sales will do. The more your people communicate with customers and prospects, the more they will sell. So, if the analytics tell us that actions are up, sales will soon follow. The delay depends on the length of your sales cycle. The communications actions are leading indicators of sales growth. Much more on this later in this chapter.

The technology system you select for your Outgrow program needs to accommodate the inputs for your participants to enter their actions on each customer interaction, and the outputs of the submitted data, in the form of a spreadsheet or comma-delimited file, which can then be manipulated in a spreadsheet. The outputs will turn into your scorecards, graphs, and data, which will be covered later in this chapter.

Tech Option #1: Your Current CRM

If you are currently using customer relationship management (CRM) software, that is one obvious tech home for your Outgrow implementation. If your system allows for some customer fields to be added, you can model your fields on the form we use in the Outgrow programs delivered by our certified Advisors. These fields are presented in detail in the coming pages. CRM software is often web based, and it tracks your customer and prospect contact information, as well as their position in your sales pipeline and the communications your team makes to them. Some common examples are:

- Salesforce

- Microsoft Dynamics 365

- HubSpot

- Zoho

- Pipedrive

The rule of thumb for your Outgrow program is: the simpler, the better. Which is why it's always better to slightly modify and use the system you already have than to add another system. It's hard enough to get people to use a single system properly and consistently. Add a second system, and your probable adoption rates drop considerably.

Technology Option #2: The Outgrow Tracking System

There are multiple options for a guided implementation of Outgrow. Please visit www.RunOutgrow.com to see if one of them fits your needs. If so, the Outgrow Tracking System will be provided to you.

Now, let's look at the Outgrow Tracking Form and its fields.

Inputs Are Captured with the Outgrow Tracking Form

The Outgrow Tracking Form is the central tech tool that Outgrowers use the most. It serves as a place to capture: the opportunities they have uncovered or progressed toward a close; the proactive action, or swings, they took to make it so; and the approximate dollar value their multi-second effort may be worth.

See page 165 for the complete Outgrow Tracking Form (OTF).

As you can see, the OTF has three parts:

1. The Opportunity Details

2. The Proactive Actions

3. The Sales Amounts

We will review each of these in Step Three below.

Outgrow Tracking Form

Your email

You will receive a record of your submission at this email.

Your Name*

Client / Prospect Type*
Current Customer

Client / Prospect Company*

Client / Prospect Contact*

Your Actions, Opportunities Discussed & F/U Plan*

Briefly describe your communications here, and the customer's response, as well as your next follow up action(s).

Proactive Actions

Proactive Call
0

Call Type
Post-Delivery Call

DYK
0

rDYK
0

Pivot to Sales or Next Conversation
0

% of Business
0

Internal Referral Request
0

External Referral Request
0

Hand-Written Note
0

Sales Growth Amounts

Enter the dollar value in ONLY ONE of the rows below: Is This a New Opportunity? A Quote or Proposal? Or a Closed Sale?

New Opportunity $ Value
If this is a new opportunity, how much it worth approximately?

Annualized Value
Enter potential annual value

Quote or Proposal Amount
If your Outgrow action resulted in a new quote or proposal, how much is it for?

Closed Amount
How much did this purchase close for?

STEP ONE: ASSIGN THE TARGET ACTIONS

At the beginning of every week, you will ask your team to make some specific quantities of communications from the list of actions detailed in the previous chapter. It almost doesn't matter which communications you ask them to make because they are all intentionally designed to grow your sales. So it's really impossible to do this part incorrectly. All of these communications will develop opportunities or move exciting opportunities forward. Nevertheless, here are some guidelines for assigning target actions.

Three Sets of Five

A good starting point for your first set of target actions is three different actions. Here is a common first assignment:

This Week's Target Actions

- 5 Proactive Phone Calls to Past Customers (They used to buy but stopped.)

- 5 DYKs

- 5 rDYKs

This allows people to double and triple up on their calls: the DYKs and rDYKs can be asked during the phone calls. So, if your Outgrower makes just five calls, they can easily rip past your action request for the week, because they can ask multiple DYKs and rDYKs on each call.

Here's another example set of actions:

This Week's Target Actions

- 5 Proactive Calls to Clients You Haven't Talked To for 6 Months or More

- 5 Quote or Proposal Follow-Ups That Are 30+ Days Old

- 5 rDYKs

In this example, you're directing your Outgrowers to make five proactive calls to a specific group of clients *and* make an additional five quote and proposal follow-ups, which are unlikely to be with the same people because the proactive calls are to clients they haven't talked to in months.

Overall, you should ask for at least five proactive calls, and at least five DYKs and/or rDYKs each week. Then you can rotate in quote or proposal follow-ups, referral requests, %Biz questions, pivots to the sale (which should really be done on *every* conversation, outgoing or incoming), and sending handwritten notes.

Be Prescriptive

The more specific you can be about who to call or which quotes to follow up on, the better this work goes. If you're asking for calls to a certain group of customers or prospects, then make sure people have easy access to the lists of their names and numbers. In the target actions above, ideally, your team has a list of customers they haven't talked to in six months or more and an easy list of quotes or proposals that are more than 30 days old. The more specific your target actions, the less wondering your people have to do about who to reach out to.

You can even be specific about your DYK request:

- 5 DYKs about the three products we are promoting this month

- 5 DYKs about our closeout products

- 5 DYKs about this specific service (In this case, they will need to ask five different customers about this one service.)

Rotate the Actions Weekly

To keep things fresh, and to work your Outgrowers through these techniques so that they gain experience and comfort with each, rotate your target action requests each time you ask. Some of my clients have a standing set of actions (for example, five proactive calls and five rDYKs) each week and then a third action slot that rotates weekly. So, depending on the week, that slot may be five quote follow-ups, or five referral requests, or five %Biz questions. This is one of the ways you can keep the work fresh.

Increase Target Action Counts Over Time

As time passes, and your team becomes more comfortable implementing Outgrow communications, feel free to increase their action counts. This is because, as detailed in the previous chapter covering all the various communications and calls, it's easy to log 6 to 10 actions per proactive call. You're only asking for 15 actions per week initially. This is set up intentionally so your Outgrowers can knock these actions out quickly and easily. For many, a couple of proactive calls on Monday will get them to your request of 15 total actions.

So, once you get to the 90-day mark of running Outgrow, it's perfectly reasonable to increase your request to 20 or 25 actions. One year in, you might target 30 actions per week. For many people on your team, this number might be covered in three to five proactive calls during the week.

Different Actions for Different Teams

If you have outside salespeople, inside salespeople, customer service people, or perhaps counter people, it's reasonable to ask each set of people to implement different Outgrow actions. For example, customer service folks are often fielding incoming calls throughout the day. For them, you might ask for fewer outbound proactive calls and ask for more DYKs, rDYKs, and pivots to the sale, all of which can easily be communicated to people who are calling in to them.

Keep it simple at first, and give everyone the same set of actions. Then, maybe 90 days in, as you and your people get more comfortable with the work, you might add a second set of actions that make sense for certain groups of your people.

Don't Worry About Assigning the Perfect Actions

With Outgrow, there is no pressure to assign exactly the right actions to your staff. All of the Outgrow Proactive Communications (OPCs) detailed in chapter 6 are helpful for revenue growth. So you don't need to ask for the perfect actions; you just need to pick a few communications that you think will help your people connect with your customers. You also don't need to call exactly the perfect customers; you just need to call some customers. You don't need to ask the perfect DYK questions; you just need to ask some DYKs. The work you deliver needs to be as close to perfect as possible, but the selling does not. The Outgrow work merely needs to be helpful.

Experiment, Assess, and Adjust—Play!

As you move from week to week, rotating actions, observe what is working particularly well and double down on those actions. If some communications are consistently *not* generating results, then try to edit them (change the scripting, for example), and if they continue to be ineffective, then you can simply do away with them. There are more than enough techniques to home in on the ones that work particularly well. So your job as the top executive or implementation executive of Outgrow at your firm is to guide your people to the most effective actions for your products or services and your customers.

SMALL OR SOLO: If you do not have a team of customer-facing people or you are the only person who sells, you can join the Outgrow Solo or Outgrow Small Business program at www.RunOutgrow.com and get your weekly target actions from a licensed Outgrow Advisor. Or you can simply lay out 10 to 15 actions per week for yourself, following the model above. Write them down and keep them in front of your eyes during the week. Put them on your calendar and set multiple alerts throughout the week to ensure that you make your proactive communications.

STEP TWO: YOUR TEAM DOES THE WORK

After you deliver your guidance for target actions, your Outgrowers go do the work. Some important points about their implementation throughout the week:

- **Outgrowers should infuse these multi-second actions into their day.** This work is absolutely not to replace their current work, but to be implemented in short bursts throughout the day as they do their other work.

- **Outgrow Asks can be done on both outbound and inbound phone calls.** Of course, the various proactive calls need to be from your Outgrower *to* the customer. But DYKs, rDYKs, pivots to the sale, pivots to the next conversation, %Biz, and referral requests can all be made on incoming phone calls as well. In fact, some of your staff, like customer service people or inside salespeople, get through the majority of their actions for the week with people who call in to them. This is an important distinction to make with your team: Outgrow is not limited to outbound phone calls. That said, it's important for *everyone*— including the inside salespeople and customer service folks—to make at least *some* proactive calls as well.

- **Five to ten minutes a day is enough.** Your people should not be doing this work for an hour per day or even 30 minutes. Rather, making and logging the Outgrow communications should take just 5 to 10 minutes per day. If it is taking longer, they are probably not doing something right.

- **Guide your Outgrowers to stack the actions.** As I demonstrated in the many examples of proactive calls in the previous chapter, Outgrowers should make multiple communications per interaction. It's easy to stack a half dozen or more OPCs per conversation, with several DYKs, an rDYK or two, and a pivot or two on every interaction.

- **Outgrow Asks can be implemented during in-person conversations.** If your Outgrowers are meeting a customer or prospect in person, they can absolutely utilize and take credit for all of the Outgrow communications like DYKs, rDYKs, and pivots. Conversations on your customers' site are terrific times to implement Outgrow.

STEP THREE: YOUR TEAM LOGS THE WORK

Now it's time to capture the proactivity your staff has implemented and the business they have opened, progressed, or closed. This is where you will either use an entry form customized within your current CRM or the Outgrow Tracking Form in a guided implementation.

OTF Part One: The Opportunity Details

Outgrow Tracking Form

Your email

You will receive a record of your submission at this email.

Your Name *

Client / Prospect Type *

Current Customer ▲▼

Client / Prospect Company *

Client / Prospect Contact *

Your Actions, Opportunities Discussed & F/U Plan *

Briefly describe your communications here, and the customer's response, as well as your next follow up action(s).

Success Of the Week!?

☐ Yes!

If you are doing this inside your own CRM, then the fields identifying the salesperson and customer will be handled by your software, and your Outgrowers won't have to enter them every time the form is filled out. But if you are using the Outgrow Tracking System, then they will have to enter these each time they fill out the form, which should take no more than 15 seconds.

The **Client / Prospect Type** field is a drop-down for Outgrowers to select the type of target they are communicating with. This will allow you to sort opportunities and progress by **Type**, which is a valuable way to organize data. For example, you will be able to quickly see if enough communications are being made to past prospects. You will also quickly know which types of customers and prospects are generating the best results.

Outgrow Tracking Form

Your email

You will receive a record of your submission at this email.

Your Name *

Client / Prospect Type *

✓ Current Customer
Past Customer
Current Prospect
Past Prospect
Cold Prospect - Have not Talked

Client / Prospect Company *

Client / Prospect Contact *

ed & F/U Plan *
re, and the customer's response, as well as your next follow up action(s).

Success Of the Week!?
☐ Yes!

Next, your Outgrower will identify the customer/prospect company and contact name.

Now to what is probably the most valuable part of the form—the **Actions, Opportunities & Follow-Up Plan**. This is where participants will *briefly* write out what they did (specifying their actions), how the customer responded, the opportunities they uncovered, and their plan to follow up. Here are a couple of examples of how to enter into this field:

Example 1:

Your Actions, Opportunities Discussed & F/U Plan*

> DYK products A, B, C. They are interested in product C. Pivoted
> to when—they said send Monday.
> rDYK what else is coming up—new construction addition
> starting in 90 days.
> Pivoted if we can meet next week, and scheduled Thursday
> 10am visit.

Example 2:

Your Actions, Opportunities Discussed & F/U Plan*

> DYK services A and B.
> rDYK what are they doing with my competition—client said
> training sessions. I offered to help with that; they are interested.
> F/U next week.
> Pivoted to service B; they need to think about it. F/U next week
> at the same time.

As you can see, the action(s) taken are identified, along with the products and services mentioned. The customer's responses are also noted, along with the follow-up actions to be done. At this point, the follow-up actions should be calendared so that they are not forgotten or lost track of.

The last piece of this section is a **Success of the Week** checkbox. If your Outgrower would like to identify this communication as one of their favorite successes this week, they can simply check this box to alert you. The Successes of the Week your participants turn in are meant to be shared with everyone involved in Outgrow, or, if you wish, company-wide. This is Step Five in the Outgrow process and will be described a bit later in this chapter.

OTF Part Two: The Proactive Actions

The second part of the form is for recording the actions and swings your people take on each interaction with customers and prospects. This is where Outgrowers log their swings. The actions logged should match up with the notes that were written in the field above.

Proactive Actions		
Proactive Call	**Call Type**	
0	Post-Delivery Call	
DYK	**rDYK**	**Pivot to Sales or Next Conversation**
0	0	0
% of Business	**Internal Referral Request**	**External Referral Request**
0	0	0
Hand-Written Note		
0		

If they made a **Proactive Call**, they would log it as one call (the maximum per interaction) and then from the drop-down menu select which type of call. The **Call Type** drop-down menu corresponds to the list of proactive calls in chapter 6.

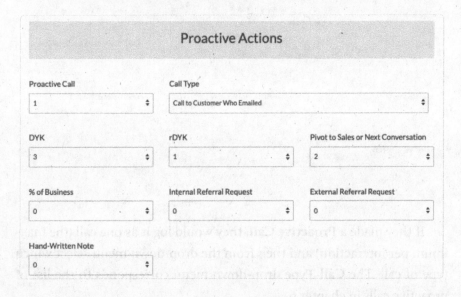

From there, your Outgrow would log the number of different communications made during this interaction.

The example above was a proactive call to a customer who emailed. On that call, the Outgrower did three **DYKs**, one **rDYK**, and two **Pivots**, for a total of seven total actions logged.

OTF Part Three: Sales Growth Amounts

Sales Growth Amounts

Enter the dollar value in ONLY ONE of the rows below: Is This a New Opportunity? A Quote or Proposal? Or a Closed Sale?

New Opportunity $ Value

If this is a new opportunity, how much it worth approximately?

Annualized Value

Enter potential annual value

Quote or Proposal Amount

If your Outgrow action resulted in a new quote or proposal, how much is it for?

Closed Amount

How much did this purchase close for?

The last part of the OTF is for dollar values. Only one of the three lines should be filled out:

- If the conversation opened up a new opportunity that is pre-quote or pre-proposal, the first line should be filled out to indicate its value on the first order and on the annualized value. For example, if the order is for a piece of equipment that costs $2,000, this should be entered into the first field, **New Opportunity $ Value**. And if you expect the customer to buy it weekly, this amount should be multiplied by 52, for a total of $104,000, which should be entered into the **Annualized Value** field.

- If the Outgrow communication resulted in a new quote or proposal, its value should be entered into the **Quote or Proposal Amount** field.

- Finally, if the communication closed new business, this dollar amount should be entered into the **Closed Amount** field.

As soon as the Outgrower submits their form, it gets added to the list of company-wide proactive activities, and a copy of the submission gets emailed to the person who entered the information, as well as their manager and, if you wish, to yourself as well. This allows powerful visibility into customer conversations on the front lines for managers, leaders, and the top executive.

Finer Points for Logging Outgrow Actions

Some nuance to help you think about logging actions, opportunities, and sales.

Log in Real Time (Not Later)

The best time to log Outgrow actions and opportunities is right after they occur, when things are fresh. The biggest value of doing so, of course, is to capture the details and nuance of the business that was opened or progressed, as well as future follow-up actions.

Sometimes, Outgrowers ask me if they can just log everything all at once at the end of the week. My response is to ask them to please list all of the details from all of the conversations they had five business days ago. Of course, they cannot. Then I ask them to tell me all the details of every selling interaction they had just *two* business days ago. Again, they cannot. Even three conversations later, it's challenging to remember what exactly happened in a particular exchange. And if they don't capture the opportunity while they remember it, where does it exist besides their fading memory? If it's not logged shortly after it occurs, there's a good chance it's gone forever.

Logging an Interaction Should Take 90 Seconds

The details entered into the **Actions, Opportunities & Follow-Up** field should be brief and shorthand. The purpose of this note is to remind the Outgrower what they are following up on, and to tell managers and leaders what actions are working. They should not be written in paragraphs. Many will start giving too much detail, and you can simply respond to them with suggestions to abbreviate their details. A line or two is enough.

Once your people get used to working with it, filling out the entire form should take no more than 90 seconds. "Get in and get out of there," I tell Outgrowers. Most people spend less than one minute entering their data.

A quick point on this: writing paragraphs in the **Opportunities, Actions & Follow-Up** field is a sign of not understanding the Outgrow program. They are trying to make up for their confusion or lack of clarity with details. Go to those people and ask if the work is clear to them. It probably isn't.

The Actions That Go into the Form Should Be Proactive Only

"Had lunch" does not need to be entered into the OTF. It's just a thing that happened. But if during lunch your Outgrower asked a couple DYKs and an rDYK, then that should definitely be entered. Even if they didn't sell anything, merely *trying to* is a swing (which they are in control of), and we are absolutely interested in counting those.

"Came to pick up order" is not a proactive action and does not need to be logged. But asking "what else do you need with that?" and "do you want to just take it now?" are excellent actions to take and log. In fact, the goal is to ask "what else?" and "when?" in every single customer interaction.

The Action Counts Logged Should Match the Note in the Actions, Opportunities & Follow-Up Field

If your Outgrower is taking credit for three DYKs, all three products and services offered should be briefly mentioned in the **Notes** field, as well as the customer's reaction. If they log an rDYK, the language used should be noted as well as the customer's response to it. We try to avoid action counts logged without any details in the **Notes** field, because the activity is unclear and difficult for the manager to understand.

Estimate the Dollar Values

The **Sales Growth Amounts** at the bottom of the form, especially on the first line, which is for pre-quote estimates, are best-guess, ballpark estimates. Some Outgrowers are uncomfortable with this at the beginning. "I don't know how much this will be," they say. "Take a shot at it," I respond. We don't need to be exact and precise. Rather, we need an educated approximation of what the numbers will be.

Why are ballparks helpful? Because you will use this information as an indicator of the impact of your Outgrow implementation. That is, the sales dollar estimates tell you if you are moving in the right direction. They inform us of the *physics*—are total opportunities growing or contracting? Your actual sales are tracked in your accounting software or another system. Those are hard facts. The Outgrow **Sales Growth Amounts** are estimates to help you understand how the work is going.

If There's a Queue of Customers, Write It Down on Paper

Some clients have counter people who work in an environment where people line up, in person, in front of them. Others have customer service people or inside salespeople who deal with one conversation after another for a while, without a break. In those situations, it's best to note your Outgrow tracking notes briefly on a piece of paper, and then enter it into the system when there is a quiet moment. So, if your participant has five interactions in a row, without a break, they can note the details in shorthand on paper and then go to the Outgrow Tracking From and enter them in one after another. If 90 seconds per entry is the maximum time requirement, they're looking at less than eight minutes to log five interactions.

How to Log Face-to-Face Conversations and Incoming Calls

If the Outgrow conversation happens in person, it can be entered once the interaction concludes. When an outside salesperson returns to their car after a meeting, for example, the Outgrow Tracking Form is accessible on any smartphone with a web browser, and can be filled out in the car before they drive away. Of course, in that scenario, the salesperson leaves the **Proactive Call** field as a "o" but fills in the **Actions, Opportunities & Follow-Up** field as normal and enters the quantity of their various swings as normal.

STEP FOUR: SHARE THE SCORECARD & ANALYTICS

What follows in this section is a comprehensive set of actual Outgrow client data, scorecards, graphs, and other analytics that Outgrow companies use. These many examples are meant to show you what is possible. Think of them as options, and go through them as ideas, to pick and choose what might work best for you.

Every Outgrow organization creates data and metrics that are uniquely their own. What's instructive or valuable to you may not help another company. Begin with the Weekly Scorecard, shown in multiple versions below, and then manipulate the data from there. Then, with time, you will develop the datasets and visual representations that are most helpful to you. Play with the metrics—they are powerful indicators of the health of your company's sales function.

Share Widely and Weekly

Share your scorecards and graphs weekly with all Outgrow participants, at minimum. At maximum, you might choose to make the information available company-wide. When you share the data with the team, you begin to close the Outgrow feedback loop. It shows the team how the company is performing in its proactive business development, and also lets each Outgrower see how their effort stacks up against that of their peers.

And make no mistake: we are tracking efforts here. Swings, not hits. The Outgrowers ranked higher on your scorecards are simply *trying* more than their colleagues. And those who are lower are trying less. The best part is these efforts are all self-reported. This is not you saying they did or didn't communicate with customers and prospects. It's them saying it. That is a very empowering position to put your team—and yourself—in: with fast, simple behaviors, they are in direct control of the strength of their sales performance, the expansion of their relationships with customers, their position on Outgrow scorecards, and their recognition among their peers.

Add Your Commentary

When you distribute the data, add some color commentary and analysis to it. Even if it's just a paragraph, your team will take great interest in your thoughts on their performance and its impact on the business. If actions are trending up, let people know that sales are about to follow. If, conversely, they are going the wrong way, you can ask them to push the gas on proactivity this week because last week wasn't great. This commentary is one of the ways you steer Outgrow within your company.

A reminder here (from chapter 3) that *you* should not be creating and manipulating the data yourself—unless it brings you joy to do so—but rather it should be served up for your commentary by an administrative person who manages the metrics on a regular basis. This person might send you the data for you to forward to the team along with your analysis.

The Outgrow Weekly Scorecard

The foundational Outgrow scorecard is a weekly view of the actions that each of your participants took and the sales growth amounts they estimate they generated. These scorecards are exported from the technology system you use into a spreadsheet like Microsoft Excel or Google Sheets. If you are working with an Outgrow Advisor, this data will be delivered to you every Monday.

Think of it like a baseball game scorecard, if you are familiar with those. It gives you a baseline view of the week and who did which actions. It also serves as a starting point for manipulating the data into whatever form and shape you wish. Here is an example of an Outgrow Weekly Scorecard:

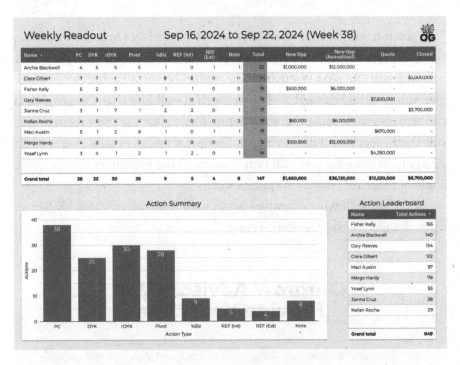

Starting with the top half of the report, we list every Outgrower and the number of actions they logged in our Tracking Form that week. You can see each person's total number of Outgrow actions, as well as their sales growth amounts on the right side of the table. On the lower left is the Action Summary, with a visual representation of how many total actions were entered. On the lower right is the running Action Leaderboard, over time. Some people call this an overall stack ranking.

The Weekly Scorecard simply contains the basics: the names of your Outgrowers, their proactive actions, and the sales growth dollars they entered. It also tells you how your Outgrow actions break down for the week and who are the overall leaders in efforts over time.

This simple but telling output gives you the basics on Outgrow outreach done over the last week.

OUTGROW SCORECARD POSSIBILITIES

This section will present a range of analytics used by Outgrow organizations. All names are intentionally obscured. My goal with this section—and with the Outgrow company case studies between each chapter—is to give you multiple examples of the powerful visibility that Outgrow data can arm you with. Most Outgrow companies customize their reporting to suit their specific and unique needs. So review what's possible here, select what might work for you, and remain open to the possibility of modifying some of these for your own application.

All of the following examples begin with the Outgrow Weekly Scorecards detailed in the previous section.

Outgrow Advisors Will Provide Your Data

Outgrow companies working with a licensed Advisor will receive Weekly Scorecards and leaderboards, as well as monthly analytics, so that you will always know *who* is participating and, critically, the results being generated. The data will be provided to you, and you will not need to create it. You will be armed with powerful leading indicators of revenue growth (more on this below).

The Stack Ranking

Here are three useful modifications to the previously presented examples of foundational Outgrow Weekly Scorecard:

The Total Weekly Actions Scorecard

Rank	Name	Week Range Total Proactive Actions
	WEEKS 41–43 (12/11–12/31) **Leaderboard**	
1	Stephen	134
2	Dan	62
3	Neely	57
4	Joseph	33
5	Mary	32
6	Brad	27
7	Sean	27
8	John	20
9	Kelly	19
10	Bernard	19
11	Morgan	19
12	Nicholas	17
13	Mika	17
14	Nicholas	17
15	Keegan	15
16	Gill	15
17	Mark	14
18	Caleb	13
19	Jason	12
20	Sarah	12
21	Joel	12
22	Jerry	11
23	Jason	9

This scorecard simply shares a total number of actions, without listing all the other details, such as which actions made up the total number. This example shows total actions over the last three weeks. You can share them weekly or biweekly.

Below is a total cumulative actions scorecard, which adds up total proactive actions submitted by each person across the total time this firm has been running Outgrow.

Leaderboard		
Rank	**Name**	**Week Range Total Proactive Actions**
1	Steve	1884
2	Stephen	1693
3	Dan	1517
4	Nicholas	856
5	Joseph	821
6	Steve	632
7	Jerry	626
8	Mike	591
9	Jason	577
10	David	571
11	Joel	568
12	Mike	567
13	Mark	565
14	Jason	558
15	Jason	486
16	Brad	486
17	Caleb	484
18	Mary	412
19	Thomas	399
20	Zach	398
21	Jennifer	392
22	Sarah	390
23	Randy	375

Average Actions per Week

Client Executive	Sum of 2-Week Average
Scott	37.5
Eric	33
John	27.5
Peter	27.5
Howard	27.5
Gary	27
James	26.5
Donald	25
Dale	24.5
Laura	23.5
Joseph	23
Bradford	21
John	19.5
Justin	19
Jesse	19
Heather	18.5
Eric	18.5
Brennan	18
Nathan	18
Brent	18
Darin	18
Carrie	18
Craig	17.5
Jordan	17.5
Jon	17.5
Timothy	17
Mike	16.5
Michael	16.5
Dwayne	16.5

This view shows the average number of actions per week over a two-week period.

The Dashboard

Week Range	Call Totals		Action Totals		
Week 1 to 38	Proactive Call 4946	Order History Call 497	DYK 4824	PreQFU 1665	Referral 582
Week Dates 03/06/23 - 11/26/23	Post Delivery Call 427	Call Customer Who Emailed 939	rDYK 3322	QFU 2120	Testimonial 709
Users 71			Pivot to Sale 1140	Percent Biz 28	Handwritten Note 98
Submissions 5315	Participation Goal Progress		Action Goal Progress		
Actions 21297	97% 0 10 20 30 40 50 60 70 80		51% 0 10000 20000 30000 40000 50000		

This Outgrow organization's dashboard provides at-a-glance action totals as well as the total number of Outgrow form submissions, total actions, participation percentages, and total actions submitted compared to target actions assigned. This view gives leadership and executives a 30,000-foot view of which actions are being implemented and where the opportunities are.

For example, the data above tells us that the %Biz questions have only been asked 28 times in 38 weeks. And only 98 handwritten notes have been sent. These are seriously low numbers compared to the other proactive communications. In this case, these two actions can be assigned as target actions for a couple of weeks, and we can observe the results they generate. The participants can be guided toward them. If they generate good results, leadership can keep asking for them to be done.

Weekly Actions Trend

The following chart is a powerful look at total actions submitted weekly, over time. Also detailed here are the total dollar values submitted in the Outgrow Tracking Form. Let's look at the last seven weeks on the chart, on the right side, where the arrows have been added. Those weeks tell two very different stories. At first the actions shoot up from 1,500 to 2,200 over a period of four weeks. During this time, we know that opportunities and sales also went up significantly. Then, suddenly, actions start to fall back down to 1,600. You can see the previous 30 or so weeks have been relatively level and stable. At the conclusion of the final week, the leader of this large professional services organization brought the decline up to all of the Outgrowers, alerting them that they needed to push the gas on proactivity because the decrease in proactivity had already led to a decrease in opportunities uncovered.

Weekly Actions by Type Trend

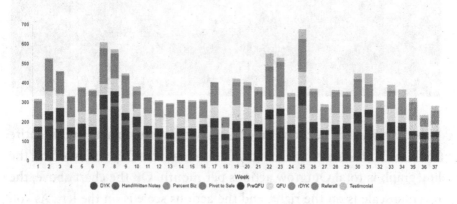

In this chart, each bar is one week of actions, company-wide, broken down by action type per the key at the bottom. This look quickly shows how many proactive actions are being submitted each week, and which direction things are heading. It also conveniently lays out exactly which actions are being focused on weekly, and how each individual action changes in quantity over time. This is a completely different firm than the trend graph above it, implementing Outgrow at a totally different time, but the last five to six weeks—which came during the end-of-year holiday period—do cause some concern. We spent a good amount of time at the start of the new year focusing on the importance of pushing the gas on proactivity, because this company's results moved in unison with their actions.

Leading Indicators of Sales Growth: Overlaying Actions with Sales

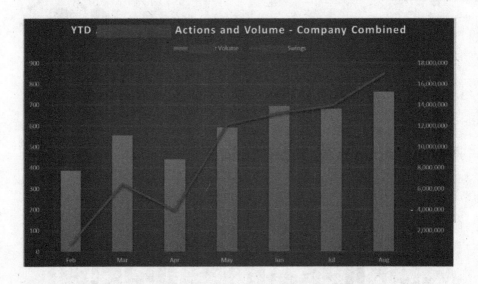

This chart and the next one may be my two favorite images in this entire book. In both charts, the bar graph is actual monthly revenue and the line graph is total Outgrow actions per month. On the chart above, the revenue scale is on the right, and the actions scale is on the left. As you can see, revenue moves in total lockstep with actions. Actions go up a lot, revenue goes up a lot. Actions go down, revenue follows. Actions go up a little, revenue goes up a little.

The previous chart is for a wholesale distributor, where product is sold very quickly, and often on the initial proactive phone call. The chart below belongs to a service company, where the sales cycle is significantly longer, with business often taking months to close. As you can see, even for the service company, sales follow actions.

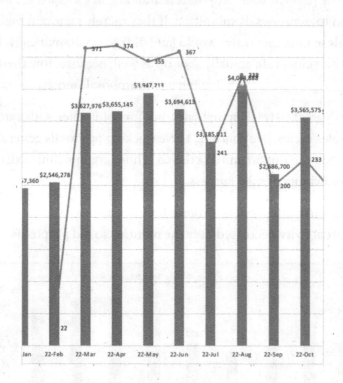

It's the same story here. When actions are high, revenue is high. When actions swing down, so do sales. Proactive communications indicate what sales will do before sales do it. And that is some incredibly powerful information to be armed with.

Quotes or Proposals Overlaid with Proactive Actions

Finally, here is a year-over-year chart for a custom-engineered product company. Their Outgrow implementation started in mid-January 2021. The graph on page 192 tracks proposals generated in 2021 versus the same month in 2020. The line graph shows the total actions submitted. Some striking takeaways:

- The jump in total proposals is dramatic. It's a 52% increase in total proposals submitted. If they merely maintain their close rate, their sales would (and did) go up dramatically. But their close rate actually shot up as well, because now their Outgrowers were following up on proposals more.

- It's great to track actual sales, but for companies with extended sales cycles, like this one, I love tracking proposals generated and even opportunities created. Those are more immediate indicators of sales success.

- Just like sales results, proposals follow actions—as the proactivity decreased over the months, so did proposals.

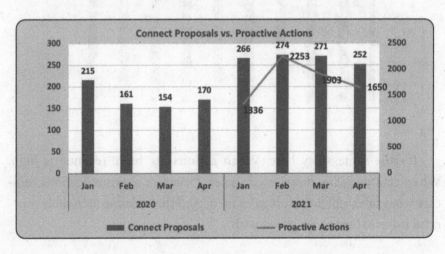

STEP FIVE: COLLECT AND SHARE THE SUCCESS STORIES

The Outgrow Tracking Form contains a small checkbox just under the **Actions, Opportunities & Follow-Up** notes field. It's labeled **Success of** the Week!? This is where your participants can tell you and their manager that *these* Outgrow Proactive Communications resulted in what they believe is a big win for them.

By marking this checkbox, the Outgrower is nominating this particular effort to be shared with the entire team. That's because, once a week, you will batch together your favorite (or all) **Success of the Week!?** submissions and share them with your team.

Share the wins you like best or actions you would like to emphasize.

The Outgrow Internal Recognition Newsletter

On page 194 is an Outgrow organization's actual recognition newsletter. Because the Outgrowers' and customers' names are detailed, I've carefully redacted them. The white spaces in the text of the document are where I removed this information. Not all Outgrow firms have such a professionally designed newsletter. Some simply send their recognition newsletter as text in an email. Here are some finer points for creating effective recognition newsletters:

- **Name names.** List the names of your Outgrowers and the customer company and individual contacts there, and identify the products discussed. This will help your people relate to the story and to their peers and colleagues.

- **Use Outgrow language.** As you can see, this firm has our Outgrow terms all over this newsletter: you can see *proactive call* mentioned several times, as well as *DYK*, *rDYK*, and *pivot to the sale*. These are swing mechanics, and when you detail *how* the sale was made, it helps everybody who reads this think about applying it to their own situations.

- **List dollar amounts where possible.** It's important to connect these short, easy efforts to real money—often, *a lot* of money.

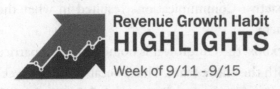

Revenue Growth Habit
HIGHLIGHTS
Week of 9/11 - 9/15

FIELD SALES ENGINEERS

Jon
Jon called customer _____ to follow up on a quote and ask if there was anything that we could do to better assist. As a result, he found that they would like to replace some of their gages and pressure switches. He used a rDYK to find out if there were any other products they purchased elsewhere that they would be interested in sourcing from us and found that they are interested in some of our panel meters. This new business opportunity offers an estimated annual total of $400,000!

Frank
Frank stopped in to speak with a potential new customer, _____ regarding our _____ water meters, to ask if they carried them and discussed how successful other distributors have been selling ours. They have decided to evaluate for this coming year, which offers a potential of $10,000 annually! In addition to this opportunity, Frank called _____ Contractors to inquire about our percent of business and how we could increase it. This gave him an opportunity to talk to them about our _____ Meter and the possibility for them to test the unit, for an estimated quote of $25,000!

Mac
Mac made a proactive call to _____ to inform them about a new manometer that they could evaluate and as a result, they requested samples of the unit to test. This could represent a $60,000 new business opportunity!

Nick
Nick placed a proactive call to _____ a potential customer that we have been attempting to schedule a meeting with for months, and successfully arranged a sales call with them for this October! Way to go!

Jonathan
While following up on a large _____ quote ($100K) with _____ Jonathan used a simple DYK and was successful in quoting an additional $8,000 of test equipment for the same job!

James
James carried out DKY/PD/PC activities to three customers: _____ and Shanghai Houxi to introduce our 6: _____ and _____ and to present value proposition of our products vs competition. He succeeded to explore potential opportunities worth $45,000.

PRODUCT MANAGEMENT

Val
Val made a Post Delivery call to _____ and received a personalized thank you for quick and courteous support.

CUSTOMER SERVICE

Melissa
Melissa's pivot to sale secured a 250 piece _____ order when she informed the customer of our upcoming price increase for a total order of $25,200! Great job!

Marcus
After rectifying a shipping mistake with an Amazon customer, Marcus sent a post-delivery follow up email to thank him for his patience and offer our assistance with any upcoming projects. In return, the customer wrote a thoughtful email congratulating _____ on its excellent customer service. We should expect to see more outcomes like this in the future!

Demian
Demian was contacted this week by _____ concerning problems with bezels getting damaged. He utilized this opportunity to use a DYK and upsell them on getting more _____ bezels and enclosures, which added $3,600 onto the order!

TECHNICAL SUPPORT

Brenden
Brenden created an estimated annual opportunity of $17,000 by using a rDYK on a _____ filtration OEM. We weren't able to assist with the customer's initial request, but after Brenden opened up the floor to our other products, the caller was very excited about our _____ and _____ Series!

Elizabeth
Elizabeth received a request from _____ for which they needed a panel meter urgently. Realizing they were in a rush, she used a DYK to offer them an _____ enclosure to go with the panel meter to reduce their install time, adding $160 to the order! Great quick thinking, Liz!

The Immense Value of Sharing Recognition

Sharing recognition, naming your most successful participants and congratulating them publicly, is one of the most effective things you can do to make change permanent. Here are just four of the many powerful benefits of sharing recognition.

- **It shows people this initiative is important to you.** By sharing the stories that your people are proudest of, you are demonstrating that you're watching, paying attention to, and reading the submissions. When making change, people only do what they believe is important to their managers. This makes it clear that your company's Outgrow implementation is a priority.

- **The people whose victories you share feel proud and enthusiastic.** You've singled them out as an example of excellent work. This is, essentially, a thank-you and a bit of bragging about their win in front of your entire crew. And in my experience with more than 250 Outgrow clients, public recognition is even more effective than financial compensation in building new behavioral habits. The reason is that commissions, and even financial incentives for maintaining action counts at a certain level, are private. Nobody else knows except the recipient. Further, the next time this person does the work you are seeking and you do not pay her, then you are unteaching the work. With this approach, the new behavior fizzles away quickly.

- **The people who didn't make the recognition list aspire to be included next time.** At more than a few of my Outgrow clients, salespeople come to the owner shortly after the recognition sharing comes out and say something like, "I submitted a great success story—why didn't I make the recognition?" I coach owners that the correct answer to this inquiry is, "Do it again next week, and I'll do my best to get you in." Making the recognition announcement is the *reason* that some people even do Outgrow at all. That's good. Whatever it takes!

- **Your recognition stories teach the work.** Instead of you or your licensed Outgrow Advisor teaching the work, sending out recognition regularly allows your participants to demonstrate the behaviors and outcomes that are most desirable. When you recognize your people, you facilitate peers teaching each other the right things to do.

And now you know all about the powerful, proven, statistically driven Outgrow system—a feedback loop for predictable revenue growth!

OUTGROW CASE STUDY: OUTGROW IS GASOLINE FOR SALESPEOPLE WHO WANT TO SELL MORE

This case study is about an individual salesperson who implements Outgrow actions in his job.

The Lumber Distribution Salesperson

Derek Houston was 26 years old when he started implementing Outgrow in his work as a lumber distribution outside salesperson. He is a seven-year veteran Outgrower, and has enjoyed tremendous financial, personal, and professional growth during this time.

When Outgrow selling was introduced at his company, East Coast Lumber, he had been working at the company for three years, and generating $2.5 million in annual sales. Seven years later, his personal sales stand at $40 million. He estimates that 95% of his total sales come from Outgrow techniques and principles.

"The fire to sell more was always burning for me," he said. "And Outgrow poured gasoline on the fire for me. It just took what I do to a new level."

He asks DYK and rDYK questions on every sales call. "Is there anything else I can be looking out for?" is his favorite rDYK. He said customers name additional products about 50% of the time he asks this question.

"I would say you can have all the natural talent and desire and the will to succeed, but having these Outgrow tools that you gave us is like the accelerant on the fire, that made my sales go BOOM!"

He also explained that he uses the powerful technique of silence multiple times a day. I asked for an example.

"I have 10 trucks of two-by-four that can hit your lumberyard today—do you want me to put these on the truck for you?"

And he stopped.

There was silence for 10 full seconds.

I am not a lumber customer, but I felt like I needed to say yes to his question!

That is the power of silence.

"What percent of the time do customers say 'yes'?" I asked Derek.

"North of 75% of my customers say YES into that silence," he answered.

This is both amazing and totally common for this technique. They're his customers, they need product, and he is simply asking to provide it.

"Being silent after pivoting to the sale helps them think about the question I just asked," he said. "It helps them digest it. And they fill the silence."

Chapter 8

THE INTERNAL MEETINGS AND CADENCE

While your team operates the Outgrow system described in the previous chapter, there is a cadence of meetings and internal interactions that's choreographed and run by the top executive or the implementation executive. If you have multiple locations, the manager of each one is in charge of these meetings. While the outbound communications are proactive actions aimed at customers and prospects, think of the meetings laid out here as *internal proactivity*. In this chapter, we will look at the daily, weekly, monthly, and quarterly rhythm of running Outgrow.

OUTGROW INTERNAL CADENC

Daily Leaders and Managers 2 Minutes	**Weekly Huddles** Managers 15-20 Minutes
• Encouragement • Short Email of Recognition • DYK Recommendation	• Review Key Metrics (2 Min) • 1 or 2 Success Stories from Last Week (3 Min) • Option 1: Review & Assign Customer Lists (10-15 Min) • Option 2: Proactive Call Planner (10-1 Min) • DYK Focus

Monthly Reviews 1-on-1 with Manager 10 Minutes	**Quarterly Planning** Managers with Group 90 Minutes
Look Back (5 Min) • Did They Swing Bat? • Meet Target Swings? • Top Results and Opportunities Created from the Month	**Look Back** • Minimum Targets Met? • Top 5 Performers • Top 5 Under-Performers
Look Forward (5 Min) • Top Wallet Share Expansion Opportunities • DYK Focus for Month • Referrals Focus for Month	**Look Forward** • Top Wallet Share Expansion Focus for the Coming Quarter • DYK Focus • Referral Focus • Pre-Quote F/U Focus • Quote F/U Focus • Top Prospect Focus

www.goldfayn.com | Copyright 2024 Alex Goldfayn

CONDUCTING THE OUTGROW ORCHESTRA

This rhythm of weekly, monthly, and quarterly connections allows you to be the conductor of Outgrow at your organization. That is, you are ensuring that your musicians are playing the right notes, at the right time. Further, you're overseeing that each section of the orchestra is playing the proper music at the right moments. Each meeting is a management opportunity that brings your guidance, encouragement, and energy and prevents your Outgrow program from becoming the Wild West.

At larger Outgrow organizations, a common concern is that multiple participants will call on the same people. This is almost never a problem, because customers are almost always happy to hear from various staff members who help them. Nevertheless, you can game-plan who will communicate with whom in these meetings, so that nobody steps on anyone's toes either internally with their teammates or externally with customers.

With these company meetings, you are planning, encouraging, motivating, and energizing your people to do the often-uncomfortable work of proactively communicating with customers and prospects. Each conversation shows your team that:

- Outgrow is important to you.

- This organic growth work is not going away. It's not a flavor of the month for you.

- You *expect* them to participate.

- In fact, it's not optional. It's simply how you sell.

- Their peers and colleagues are doing it and seeing tremendous success.

Also, and perhaps most important, each of the weekly, monthly, and quarterly Outgrow meetings detailed here extract your people from their constant reactive problem-solving customer service work. This time allows them to plan their proactivity, which is impossible to do in the midst of their regular high-stress, reactive customer service efforts.

OUTGROW DAILY MENTIONS
(TWO MINUTES A DAY)

As your team implements their daily actions, and you receive the details in your email via the Outgrow Tracking Form or in your CRM, you can touch base with them briefly by sharing:

- An encouraging word in person.

- A short email of thanks about an Outgrow activity they submitted.

- An email or in-person tip or idea based on their submission, for example:
  - "This seems like a good opportunity to ask an rDYK and pivot (what else, and when)."
  - "Don't forget to follow up on that big quote with company xyz."

You can also suggest DYK products or proactive calls in your regular conversations with your colleagues. These little daily touch points are gentle feedback and motivation for your team's Outgrow work. You are reminding them that you are interested in their work on this important effort to intentionally and proactively grow sales.

THE OUTGROW WEEKLY HUDDLE
(20 MINUTES ON MONDAYS)

The 20-minute Outgrow Weekly Huddle (OWH) is one of the key management tools in an Outgrow organization. They're fast, packed with proactive productivity, and avoid complaining and negativity at all costs. If somebody brings a customer problem to the table, ask them to hold it until the meeting is over, and discuss it then. The Outgrow Weekly Huddle is for opportunities, not problems. The meeting consists of the following components.

A Quick Review of Your Key Metrics (Two Minutes)

Key metrics can include:

- Total actions submitted last week, noting if they are up or down over the week before.

- Participation percentage among your team—how many contributed at least 5 actions (a single call with a few Outgrow actions) or 10 actions.

- Proposal or quote counts, product sales volume (quantity, length, or weight), and/or sales dollars closed last week, noting if they are up or down over the week prior. We are looking for the most important short-term indicators of your sales success. If you have a fast sales cycle, you can use actual dollar sales and quote quantity. For longer sales cycles, you might count proposals written and also, perhaps, focus on follow-ups made.

Share One or Two Top Success Stories from the Last Week (Three Minutes)

Come prepared with one or two of your favorite submissions that were marked Success of the Week by your Outgrowers, and ask the participants to (briefly) tell their own stories. This recognizes their good work and results, and also teaches their colleagues what is working. It has the added benefit of helping to bring along people who might be resisting or avoiding the work (more on this in the next chapter).

During the success sharing, name the customer and the specific actions taken ("I made a proactive call to follow up on a quote, which closed on the spot, and then I asked an rDYK about what projects are coming up that I can help with, and they said . . ."). If people don't describe the actions taken, ask them to be specific. This focuses everyone on the swing mechanics, and further immerses everyone in the details of the proactive work of Outgrow.

Option 1: Review Customer Lists (10 Minutes)

There are two options here, and you can alternate them, move between them, or just go with the one that feels good to you in the moment.

Come to the Weekly Huddle armed with one or more of the customer lists detailed in chapter 4. You might go over the list of customers with outstanding quotes or proposals that need a follow-up, and assign the follow-ups in the meeting to individual Outgrowers so that there is no doubt about who should follow up with whom.

You might go over a Zero Dark 30 list of customers who haven't bought much in the last month. Or perhaps you name a bunch of customers on the list of Customers Who Used to Buy but Stopped. Talk about the buyers on the list(s) you choose and then, again, quickly assign them to the individuals at the meeting. The list you select to discuss and assign matters not. All that matters is that your Outgrowers are armed with a list of customers or prospects they can make proactive calls to.

There is time here to discuss the people being assigned to Outgrowers. What have your people heard about this customer? Is she working on something interesting? What else does she probably need? Encourage people to write down additional names during the discussion if they think of other people to call.

OUTGROW PROACTIVE CALL PLANNER

My Best Customers Who Can Buy More	Customers Who Used to Buy but Stopped

My Smaller & Medium Customers Who Can Buy More from Me	Customers Who Recently Received Products or Services – Follow Up

Customers I Haven't Talked to in 3 Months or More	PROSPECTS – I Am Having Active Conversations With – Follow Up

PROSPECTS – I Once Talked to but They Did Not Buy – Follow Up	PROSPECTS – I Know Are Buying Elsewhere

Option 2: Use the Proactive Call Planner

As an alternative to the list review, consider using the 10 minutes to do the customer lists this way (perhaps every other week).

Pass around a proactive call planner to each attendee, and give them two minutes to write down as many names as they can. They can go to their emails, text messages, quotes list, or any other reference. Direct them to the places that will help them recall names. Their customers can be written in many, a few, or just one of the categories on this list. In two minutes, people can often write down more than 10 names.

Then you can use the remaining eight minutes to let people go read off the names on their lists, while the others at the table listen and comment. Encourage reactions and feedback during the discussion. You might hear reactions like, "That customer came in the other day and bought products X and Y." Or, "That reminds me—how long has it been since we talked to this other customer?" The idea is to proactively consider and discuss people who can buy more. Encourage people to write down additional names while they listen to the discussion and fill in their planner further.

Reiterate Your Target Actions for the Week

With their customer calls assigned and their proactive call planners filled out, reiterate your target actions and quantities for the week, and remind people that they should call 5, or 10, or whatever your preferred number of customers is from the list.

Now, they won't wonder who to call. They won't worry about calling exactly the right customers. They have their lists. You've prescribed the customers to reach out to, or they've simply made their written plan.

Now it's time to go help more people this week!

THE OUTGROW MONTHLY REVIEW (FOR MANAGERS: 10 MINUTES PER OUTGROWER)

The Monthly Review is done individually, with managers meeting with each of their Outgrowers one-on-one, for no more than 10 minutes each. If you are the top executive and the implementation leader, you are having these meetings with your frontline, customer-facing Outgrow participants. For larger companies, your managers have these meetings with each Outgrower on their team, and you meet to discuss the results with managers.

The key for these meetings is for each Outgrower to send their manager the details on this Monthly Review form in advance of your meeting. At a minimum, they should come to the meeting with this form filled out and submitted. There are paper versions and a digital submission form in the Outgrow Tracking System.

The Outgrow Monthly Review meeting consists of a five-minute look back and a five-minute look forward (see pages 209–210). Because it's so short, it can be added to another conversation you are having. It's important for the Outgrower to come prepared to this meeting, particularly with the details on the top half of the form, looking back at the previous month.

The Look Back details include:

- Did I swing the bat and make proactive communications?

- Did I meet the target communications number?

- A list of top results for the month, including their three favorite opportunities opened, opportunities progressed forward, and those that were closed. You are asking for their Top 3 in each of these categories.

The Look Forward details include:

- Top Wallet Share Expansion priorities this month, including the customer name, how to expand volume on current products or services sold, which products and services can be added, and internal referral opportunities.

- DYK product and service priorities.

- Referral focus and priorities: the customers likely to have additional internal buyers and who should be asked for a referral to a buyer at another firm.

This meeting sends each of your participants into a new month of Outgrow proactivity with some guidelines and expectations so that they are not wondering who to call and what to ask about.

THE OUTGROW QUARTERLY PLANNING MEETING (90 MINUTES EVERY THREE MONTHS)

The Outgrow Quarterly Planning Meeting is 90 minutes long and is designed to be attended by leadership and all customer-facing participants.

Outgrow Quarterly Look Back

The look back is for you or your leaders to think about and prepare.

See pages 211–212. The first two yes or no questions are the same across all three meetings—weekly, monthly, and this Quarterly Planning session: Did your team swing the bat, and did the group meet your minimum target action count? The next two sections are to be prepared in advance, before the meeting.

Top Outgrow Performers: Now I'd like you to go to the scorecards and data, and identify your top performers. Have they been recognized among the team? If not, the quarterly meeting is a great time to do so. Have they been otherwise incentivized or rewarded?

OUTGROW MONTHLY REVIEW

One-on-One

Look Back at Last Month

st and discuss Outgrower's top results from the last 30 days.

anager Name: _____   **Date:** _____

utgrower Name: _____

d you take proactive action?   Y / N

d you reach minimum swings?   Y / N

Outgrow Results from Last Month		
New Opportunities Opened	Opportunities Progressed	Closed
1.		
2.		
3.		
4.		
5.		
6.		
7.		
8.		
9.		
10.		

Outgrower's KPIs from Last Month				
# of New Opportunities Opened	$ Opened	# of Quotes/Proposals Sent	$ Quote/ Proposed	$ Closed

OUTGROW MONTHLY REVIEW

One-on-C

A Look Forward to This Month

Review Outgrower's top opportunities, priorities, DYKs, and referral requests for the coming month.

Outgrower's Top Opportunities For This Month		
Customers/Prospects	DYK Products and Services	Next Action(s)
1.		
2.		
3.		
4.		
5.		
6.		
7.		
8.		
9.		
10.		

This Month's DYK Focus

This Month's Referral Focus	
Internal	External

OUTGROW QUARTERLY PLANNER

Look Back At Last Quarter

t and discuss Outgrower's top results from the last quarter.

d we swing the bat?   Y / N

d we meet minimum actions?   Y / N

Top Performers		
Name	Recognized?	Incentivized/Rewarded?

Under Performers		
Name	Buy-In Possible?	Buy-In Plan?

OUTGROW QUARTERLY PLANNER

A Look Forward to Next Quarter
Outgrow top priorities for the next 90 days.

We Will Proactively Expand Wallet Share With		
1.	4.	7.
2.	5.	8.
3.	6.	9.

We Will Focus on These DYKs		
1.	4.	7.
2.	5.	8.
3.	6.	9.

We Will Ask for Referrals From		
1.	4.	7.
2.	5.	8.
3.	6.	9.

We Will Make Pre-Quote or Pre-Proposal Follow-Ups To		
1.	4.	7.
2.	5.	8.
3.	6.	9.

We Will Follow Up on These Quotes or Proposals		
1.	4.	7.
2.	5.	8.
3.	6.	9.

Top Underperformers: List the people who underperformed your expectations, perhaps even surprising you. Then answer two questions for each person: Do you believe buy-in is possible for each of them (your instinct will probably be correct here), and if so, what is the buy-in plan? A one-on-one conversation? A public analysis of the data and why some people are not participating? Perhaps you or each person's manager can check in with them weekly for a kind of performance improvement plan? Additional techniques for buy-in will be covered in the next chapter.

Looking Forward: Outgrow Priorities for the Next 90 Days

The following planning should be with your entire customer-facing team, in a 90-minute meeting. The Six Outgrow Focuses should be examined and discussed as a team, category by category and customer by customer. These focus areas are designed to spark rich conversation. Someone should scribe the items as they are being discussed, and a summary report should be circulated to all in attendance for reference after the meeting.

- **Wallet Share Expansion focus**—reviewing the top opportunities to sell more to your current customers.

- **DYK product or service focus**—identifying the offerings you want your people to concentrate on over the coming months.

- **Referral focus**—identifying who should be asked for internal and external referrals.

- **Pre-quote or proposal follow-up focus**—identifying the top opportunities to move toward a quote or proposal this quarter.

- **Quote or proposal follow-up focus**—listing the most important quotes and proposals that need following up next quarter.

Here are the time requirements for these meetings that drive Outgrow at your company:

- Weekly Huddles: 20 minutes per week, which add up to about 17 hours over 52 weeks.

- Monthly Reviews: 10 minutes per Outgrower for your managers. If a manager has these with 10 customer-facing reports (likely on the high side, per manager), this is 100 minutes a month, or 20 hours per year.

- Quarterly Planning Meetings: 90 minutes each, for a total of 6 hours per year.

This totals up to 43 total hours annually, or about 50 total minutes per week, split across multiple leaders and managers. That's less than one hour per week to plan, organize, and energize systematic and predictable 20% annual revenue growth, year after year. That, my friends, is time very well spent.

CUSTOMIZE, EXPERIMENT, PLAY

The content and topics I laid out for these meetings are starting points and reference points. Begin with these, and then customize so that each session suits your unique business needs. Outgrow companies cover the items I list, but they also tweak, evolve, edit, experiment, and fine-tune over time. Try things. Play around with ideas and concepts. The point with all of these interactions is to (1) put you in control of your Outgrow implementation, (2) allow you to be prescriptive in the communications you ask for in terms of customers and prospect targets as well as products and services being communicated, and (3) give your team dedicated time and space to think proactively instead of reactively. Steer these meetings in the direction that works best and makes the most sense for your company!

OUTGROW CASE STUDY: A COMMON BUSINESS DEVELOPMENT LANGUAGE

IMEG is a large engineering services company with more than 80 teams around the United States, and over 2,800 engineers between them. They've been running Outgrow for five years, and have more than 600 people—senior leaders, division leaders, client executives, project managers—running it.

The most telling chart of their journey is this one, which shows the impact of Outgrow in the early months of their implementation.

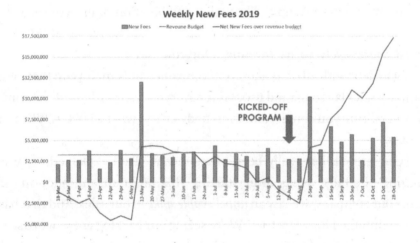

Each bar is a week of new fee sales, and the horizontal line was their weekly sales goal. The line graph is their new fees over or under that budget. It illustrates how far above or below their goal they are, cumulatively.

As you can see, Outgrow was launched in mid-August; most weeks leading up to that point were below their budget goal, and their cumulative new fees were about $2.5 million below their goal. After starting Outgrow, their new fees took off in dramatic fashion, with nearly every week being significantly above budget. The company added $20 million in 10 weeks to their net new fees over budget. One of the most interesting aspects to this growth is that engineering project sales take a long time to open, progress, and close. These are long sales cycles. And yet, with hundreds of people communicating with thousands of clients, sales had no choice but to shoot up, even in a business with a very long sales cycle.

What caused this sudden change?

IMEG's CEO, Paul VanDuyne, analyzed the change this way: "Our people never understood how much they meant to clients. Outgrow provided them with confidence. We realized we're not selling, we're helping. Our people have embraced this, and these are people who thought, *I will never be a salesperson.* And they've embraced it because with Outgrow they're *not selling*, they're helping. It's a *huge* mindset change."

When IMEG started running Outgrow, it had 1,200 engineers. Today, that number is over double. Through a combination of growth through acquisition and proactive selling for organic sales increases, IMEG has added aggressively to its revenue. Outgrow has given the company a strong benefit with all of its acquired companies and employees: there is a common sales language and process for everybody, regardless of the company or culture you come from. Everybody knows what a DYK, rDYK, and Pivot is.

"Our growth has really been phenomenal," Paul explained. "It was amazing—literally weeks after starting this program and adopting it across our company, we saw an *unbelievable spike* in our sales. And that has been maintained for years now. We're seeing our backlog grow; we're seeing our sales grow. It has been an unbelievable boost to us as a company."

Chapter 9

THE CHALLENGES AND OBSTACLES

At this point in the book, the entire Outgrow system for predictable organic revenue growth has been laid out. You know how to create the right mindset internally; you've identified the staff members who can create significant new sales for you in short bursts daily; you and your teams understand the importance of customer lists; you've learned the three specific ways to easily expand wallet share; you have the communications techniques you will be asking your team to make; you've seen the five-step feedback loop for assigning, implementing, tracking, reporting, and recognizing Outgrow work; and you know the quarterly, monthly, weekly, and daily meeting cadence that choreographs your implementation and drives Outgrow forward within your company.

Now it's time to look at the most common obstacles, challenges, and

217

resistance items that Outgrow organizations experience, and how to overcome them. I've personally done this work with more than 400 companies in many different industries, across categories including manufacturers, wholesale distributors, and professional services companies. I can tell you from this experience that the challenges and resistance points are consistent. They repeat, regularly, regardless of company size, industry, or leader.

This is so because we are creating thinking and behavior change in human beings, who almost universally do not enjoy change. Further, the change we are trying to make involves adopting behaviors that people have a lot of fear and discomfort with. As discussed, fear is the strongest emotion, and we will do nearly anything to avoid rejection, making the *fear of rejection* incredibly difficult to overcome. The Outgrow program will overcome this fear successfully for many, but not all, of your team members.

So let's examine the buy-in percentages, the most common resistance points you can expect from your people, and the challenges you may come across during your Outgrow work. Of course, I'll do my best to detail how to address each challenge.

BUY-IN AND PARTICIPATION

Initially, the typical Outgrow participation breaks down like this:

- Approximately one-third of your people will be enthusiastically bought in and participating. This group of customer-facing people is hungry, more aggressive in their sales-related work, and interested in growth. They tend to be interested in making more money (not everybody is) and helping your organization attain its targets.

- Another one-third will be somewhere between less than fully committed and wait-and-see mode. They might do some of the proactive actions you request, but not all of it. They may have one foot in the Outgrow world, with the other foot still comfortably entrenched in their reactive problem-solving world. Or they might simply sit back, look around, and observe what everyone else is doing while deciding what they will do. It's possible to bring along nearly all of the people in this group into the first group, and gain their complete buy-in over time. Not all of them, but almost all of them.

- The final third are unlikely to ever come along with your initiative, no matter how hard you try. All the layers of Outgrow—target action assignments, tracking, scorecards, public internal recognition, and even financial incentives—are unlikely to work. The people in this group are particularly set in their ways. They've often been with your company for a very long time. And they have a particularly intense discomfort with change and new things. If just one or two of the people in this group surprise you and buy in, consider that a significant victory.

Within six to twelve months, your participation will settle into the 50 to 60% range of all customer-facing employees. This is what's typical. Some Outgrow firms are higher, others are lower, but they all add significantly to their sales.

All Outgrow organizations add significantly to their sales directly from this effort. As presented, across the hundreds of firms that run Outgrow, the average growth is 20 to 30% annually. But almost none of these companies have 100% participation. As with most things, much of the growth is created by only some of the people. So, even if you only get the average participation of 50 to 60%, and you follow the Outgrow system, you should still expect significant sales growth. If you use an Outgrow Advisor, you will be on the higher end of this growth range. But even if you self-implement, you will see significant intentional sales being added regularly—as long as your people are proactively communicating on a consistent basis.

COMMON RESISTANCE AT THE START OF YOUR OUTGROW WORK

The top causes of staff resistance have already been identified: intense fear of rejection and "forced change," which is often interpreted as more work without more pay. Most people don't like change because it moves them away from habits they've long been comfortable with into those that are much less comfortable.

There's more.

Most people have a career of experience watching new initiatives fail. New corporate efforts tend to come on strong and then fizzle away. This is because permanent change is very difficult to make at companies. Staff is much better at making new things go away than leadership is at making them stick. Making things go away is much easier work! Simply avoiding it and *waiting* is often enough. *If I wait it out long enough, then this, too, shall pass.* And it almost always does.

Your people don't believe Outgrow is different from those other efforts. They think this initiative—indeed, *any* new initiative—is likely a passing fad.

You're starting your change effort behind the 8-ball. Luckily, Outgrow comes with layers of safety nets, including detailed accountability, score-carding, and recognition, that help overcome this reality and help cement it as a permanent change at your company.

What follows are the resistance points we frequently hear from individual Outgrowers, along with how to react to them. After working with more than 400 clients over 20 years, these are the concerns and pushbacks that come up repeatedly. One important observation I'd like to include here is that these are almost always *honest.* That is, your employee truly feels this way. They are expressing their fears and discomforts with changing (even if only slightly, for a minute or two) how they do their work. So don't assume dishonesty and some ulterior motive. It does happen, but it's a tremendous exception.

For each resistance point, I will briefly explain *why* your salespeople may raise it and take a quick look at the psychology and concerns behind it. I'll also help with a response that has proven effective (and even share one or two that were *not* so effective), so that you are able to react in a way that helps your people and your Outgrow implementation.

"I'm Already Doing This"

Welcome to one of the most common reactions by staff who aren't enthusiastic about new pursuits. "I already do this" is frequently heard from more experienced salespeople. It's true that they talk to their customers a lot, but, as we've established, it's often a reactive, customer-service conversation. When it's not customer service, it's order-taking, or lunch, or golf, or fishing. What it tends *not* to be, almost universally, is intentional, proactive, organic Wallet Share Expansion and sale growth. You will probably hear this upon introducing the program to your team. But once they start to go through the communications, your people will realize they were *not*, in fact, already doing this work.

Why They Say It

This common response is a result of several thought processes. Each person can be affected by one or a combination of the following:

- They do not clearly understand what Outgrow efforts are. They figure they talk to customers all day, every day, and probably don't need to do so more. It hasn't completely registered yet that Outgrow work is intentional business expansion, question by question, customer by customer.

- They are threatened. Taking on a new sales growth program implies that your salespeople are not performing as well as they can be. "I'm already doing this" is their defensive way to justify their work and value to you.

- Salespeople often confuse *thinking* about doing something a lot and actually doing it. You know, thinking about something for a long time and avoiding it—extended procrastination—is taxing, energy-consuming work. It feels challenging and complicated, and it's particularly tiring. So, many times, people *think* about asking a customer for a referral for a long time—*years, perhaps*—but never do. This work of constantly thinking about it and avoiding it can easily be mixed up with actually asking for referrals.

- They simply don't want to do more work, and are seeking to avoid it by telling you this new program is unnecessary.

How to Respond

In my early years of doing this work, I would debate and disagree with their assessment. I would confront and challenge. "Oh, that's great. How many referrals do you ask for monthly? Not those that come in to you, but how many do you request from customers?" This would prove my point, but would only serve to make the (non)participant even more defensive. So, that's not the best way to go. Instead, I quickly moved toward a version of the following nonconfrontational response to "I'm already doing it."

"That's great. Now we will all do these things, together, in a systematic way over time."

Emphasize the system, and all the team members focusing on Outgrow activities together as a unit.

This disarms the resistance and reminds your resister that they are a part of a larger team and you expect them to come along with the group.

"We're So Busy, I Don't Have Time to Do This"

Another common early resistance, and a quite accurate one: your people are busy. They're not sitting around waiting for the phone to ring. They are solving one problem after another, jumping through customer hoops, doing tremendous—probably world-class—customer service work, in addition to taking orders, determining pricing, and maybe even writing and sending quotes and proposals and then following up on them internally to make sure everything is shipped on time or the services are properly delivered. That's super-extra busy.

Why They Say It

Because it's true, and they feel the fatigue of the typical day I describe above. They've also been through change initiatives, and maybe even sales programs or trainings, that demand a lot of time to implement. Many selling programs tear down what you do now and replace it with a whole new way of going to market. This isn't that, at all. It's the opposite: Outgrow doesn't seek to replace anything you're already doing. Rather, it seeks to infuse and inject proactive questions and approaches that individually take moments of their time to execute.

How to Respond

There are a few ways to effectively respond to this resistance.

- "I know how busy you are, which is why we selected Outgrow to begin with. It only requires a few minutes of attention per day."

- "We don't have to change anything about how we serve our customers. Outgrow is just about consistently helping them a little bit more."

- A little firmer: "Do you have five minutes available today? That's all this takes."

"How Can We Possibly Handle More Work?"

This fear stems from worry over the increase in work once they sell more. Who will deliver it? We talk about the sales work requiring only a few minutes daily. But the *doing and delivering* of what is sold takes significantly longer. Your people are thinking about how hard and how much they work today, and, naturally, more sales means more work for everyone. It's a fear of success, essentially.

Why They Say It

Because many people rightly feel like they are so busy that they are drowning and only rarely have time to come up for air. They assume that additional Outgrow sales will only make them busier.

How to React

Here are some helpful ways to respond to this resistance:

- "We won't expect *you* to do it all."

- "In fact, as the business grows, we will need to promote people to manager positions. This means your role and your pay will grow."

- "Let us worry about staffing up to deliver the growth we will attain."

"I Can See How This Can Help the Inexperienced Salespeople, but It's Not for Me"

This resistance acknowledges that there is value in the work for the company, for customers, and other salespeople, but not for the resister. *It's good for the new guys, but not me.* This comes up frequently from veteran and experienced salespeople. They state that the inexperienced and less successful can benefit, but this is not work they need to be doing at their level.

Why They Say It

The reasoning behind this resistance is layered. First, they acknowledge to you, the owner or their manager, that there is value in the proactive communications work, so they aren't *actually* resisting, from their perspective. Second, by saying (not even implying) that they are too experienced and successful to benefit from additional communication to customers and prospects, they elevate their own work and effort, boosting both their own ego and the visibility of their value. Third, they create distance between themselves and the "less experienced," thereby pushing those folks down. If all this feels very cynical, that's because it is. Experienced and long-tenured salespeople often develop—and unload onto you—a significant dose of cynicism.

How to React

Here are some ways to respond to this type of resistance:

- "This isn't a remedial training program. It helps all levels of salespeople sell more by showing up more, following up more, and asking for more work or orders."

- "Outgrow is a little bit different than other sales programs because it isn't a training program, but a *doing* program. I know you know these things, but now we're going to do them all together, in a systematic way."

- "Those newer salespeople look to you for leadership and example. Outgrow will put you in a position to be a player-coach in a way. They would certainly benefit from hearing about your success with this work!"

COMMON RESISTANCE DURING THE (PERMANENT) IMPLEMENTATION PHASE OF OUTGROW

You can expect to hear some of the following resistance items throughout your ongoing implementation of the Outgrow system.

"I'm Doing It; I'm Just Not Writing It Down"

A central component of Outgrow is tracking proactive efforts and opportunities. Humans, by rule, tend not to like or appreciate being tracked. It's accountability, often for people who have worked without much accountability for a long time. It's also a little (tiny) bit of additional work on top of the communications. As I stated in chapter 7 where we looked at how to quickly log Outgrow communications, or swings, the logging piece should take less than 90 seconds after each Outgrow customer interaction.

Why They Say It

They say this to do less work! It's an extra bit of recordkeeping after each proactive conversation with a customer. It's possible that it can get tedious if somebody logs *many* interactions a day, but most people will only enter two or three or four a day. So, that's two or three or four minutes.

How to React

Here are some ways to respond to this pushback:

- "If you are doing the work, you deserve the credit. It's not fair if you're making proactive calls, asking DYKs, rDYKs, and following up but not being recognized for it on the scorecards or in the success stories we share."

- "I would like to see and hear about your good work, and hear about your success."

- "If you don't log the opportunity, how can we follow up on it? Where does it exist if it's not in the Outgrow system?"

- "Outgrow arms us with really accurate leading indicators of our future sales growth. Without your activity in the system, we no longer have a complete or accurate picture and the data becomes much less useful."

"Do You Want Me to Log Notes or Sell?"

A close cousin to the previous resistance point, this one seeks to elevate the importance of the act of selling while simultaneously minimizing the importance of recordkeeping, as though the latter is not a part of the former. It's a somewhat creative—if confrontational—effort to avoid tracking actions, which uses the leadership's drive for growth against them.

Why They Say It

Simply, to avoid logging and tracking, and the accountability that comes with it. There's also an element of "these customers and relationships are mine," and tracking the relationship-building communications makes it less so. Especially in companies where there has never been much sales accountability—which is most companies—we see a push against logging and tracking behaviors and results.

How to React

In response to this resistance, you can say things like:

- "I'd like you to sell proactively and for you to track what happened for less than a minute per customer interaction."

- "Actually, logging proactive actions *is* a part of selling."

- "I'd like your participation in this program. It's important to us."

"I've Already Called Everyone I know; I Can't Think of Anyone Else."

This is a very common concern expressed by newer Outgrowers who are two to three months into their proactive outreach to customers and prospects. They simply feel like they've already called everyone they know and that there is nobody left. This feedback isn't really resistance as much as it is asking for help. With this question, your people are asking what they should do next.

Why They Say It

There is particularly interesting psychology behind this one, and it revolves around the following areas:

- Usually, they haven't proactively called everybody they know, but rather, everybody they talk to on a regular basis or at least semi-regularly. These are the only people who are easy to think of because they are in our minds. It's a lot harder to think about people you haven't talked to.

- Because Outgrowers have been mostly reactive in their work until *this work*, their brains haven't had much practice thinking of people to call who they *don't* talk to regularly. If you've never driven a car on a public road, you need guidance and practice before you get comfortable with it. The same thing is true with proactive phone calls.

- The fears and discomforts described at length in chapter 2 play a huge role here. They could just as easily be saying "I've called everybody I am comfortable calling, and there's nobody left."

How to React

Here are some ways to approach this call for help from your Outgrowers.

- First, be sure to have customer and prospect lists at the ready for your Monthly Reviews, which are one-on-one, and for your Weekly Huddles with your team. (Reminder: these meetings are laid out in detail in chapter 8 and the customer lists are described in chapter 4.) Discussing the lists in your meetings and actively assigning the names to your Outgrowers is a direct solution to this issue. It removes the mental energy that your team must spend thinking about—perhaps agonizing over—who to call.

- "Where can you go to find the customers and prospects you spoke to more than 6 or 12 months ago?"

- "Remember that we know more than one person at our customers' companies. Who else can you be calling and checking in with at each customer?"

- "How about asking your customers for an internal referral— about who else buys our services or products there who we can help?"

- "If you've called them all over the last two or three months, then it's reasonable to check in with them again. Their needs change all the time. For some of our customers, they need our products and services for new jobs *every day*."

- "The good news is that Outgrow action can be done on incoming phone calls. You can ask DYKs, rDYKs, %Biz questions, and referral requests—among other items—on calls that come in to you. In fact, you can log two simple actions on every single incoming call by asking 'what else?' and 'when?' questions. This is an rDYK and a pivot."

"I Won't Bring Up Products and Services I Don't Know Anything About"

A significant part of Outgrow is to ask DYK questions about products and services that the customer is not currently buying. These actions are incredibly effective—as I've stated elsewhere, the statistics on many millions of DYKs asked, logged, and tracked over nearly two decades inform us that 20% of these questions turn into a new line of business. So, if your people simply ask five DYKs on a call—which can take 10 to 15 seconds—one should close in time.

However, as you now know, human behavior is determined by avoiding that with which we are not comfortable. And almost every Outgrower is uncomfortable suggesting products and services that they either (1) don't have much experience with, or (2) have not suggested frequently in the past.

Why They Say It

This pushback results from fear. Customer-facing people fear being asked questions they don't know the answers to. They don't want to be embarrassed. They don't want to look like fools. They fear their customers will think less of them. They are afraid *you* will think less of them if they can't answer some questions about a product or service you offer.

The rather significant problem with all this is if Outgrowers only bring up products they know intimately, there is likely a large proportion of your offerings that is never being discussed with your customers. I have some wholesale distribution clients running Outgrow that have tens of thousands of products. How many do you think a salesperson can store in their active recall memory? Fifty? Maybe 100? Now let's narrow it down to how many of those 50 to 100 products they are comfortable with. You are left with only an infinitesimally small percentage of products that are actually being discussed with customers.

How to React

Consider the following responses to this type of resistance.

- "You don't need deep knowledge about every product or service you ask a DYK about. We're just planting seeds here, alerting our customers what they can buy from us."

- "If they need more details, simply offer to connect them to somebody who knows the details. Customers will appreciate and respect that. Nobody will look down on you for that. Just the opposite!"

- "Keep our line card, or offerings list, in front of your eyes, and simply mention two or three items in each conversation."

- "You don't need to ask about the perfect DYK product or service—or even the ones you know the most about. You just need to ask DYK questions. We're just helping the customers, educating them."

"I Haven't Worked for 10 Years with This Customer to Risk Losing It All by Sending Him to This Other Guy on This Other Team"

This is a cross-selling concern related to referring a customer to another salesperson, or in the professional services space, another seller-doer. DYK questions are cross-selling offers, and if your company is large enough, the salesperson for this other product or service is on another (unfamiliar) team. They may not even know each other. Of course, cross-selling additional products and services is a large part of your opportunity to grow business with each customer.

In my experience with Outgrow clients, the *most* worried cross-selling resisters become its greatest advocates when the customer comes back satisfied—and they do exactly that just about every single time. The resister is further rewarded when they receive cross-selling business from their colleagues in return. It's a win-win-win—the customer is happy, the referring salesperson has done a strong favor for the customer and gains more business from that customer and others who are sent over, and the receiving salesperson is thrilled with the additional business.

Why They Say It

Here's that word again: the resisting salesperson *fears* a negative experience for their customer, caused by another employee, thereby jeopardizing everything they've worked for. It's very uncomfortable for them to turn over their hard-earned customer, an account carefully maintained and serviced by them. What if the other salesperson screws it up and the customer leaves? Or if it doesn't work out, the customer will be angry and express their anger and displeasure to the referring salesperson, who owns the relationship.

There is also an element of possessiveness at play here. *This is my customer—why would I risk turning them over to you?* It's a common mindset among salespeople, as the best among them consider themselves a mini entrepreneur of sorts. Like entrepreneurs, they don't get paid unless they sell something, and so, like entrepreneurs, it takes significant risk to do the job. So their thinking is totally understandable, and even *reasonable*, but this position is an obstacle to your business growth, and should be actively challenged. Here's how.

How to React

Consider responding to this resistance in one of the following ways.

- "Once you start sending business to another team, they almost always actively work to return the favor to you."

- "Everybody wins in this situation: your customer gets to benefit from additional help from us; *you* look good and will get more business from this customer and others; and the recipient of your connection to your customer will benefit from the new work."

- "We are trying to sell more. This is a big way to do it, and as a direct result *you* will sell more."

POTENTIAL CHALLENGES

Here are three common challenges and potential pitfalls you may come across during your Outgrow work. Be on the lookout for the following.

Managers Who Don't Lead Their Teams Through Outgrow

As I've mentioned elsewhere, your managers—leaders of teams—have the most impact on the success of your Outgrow implementation. The team goes as their leader goes. If a manager is not supportive of this work, their entire team is unlikely to run Outgrow. If one or two people on that team do make proactive communications because they want to support the company's goals and direction, they will be doing so in spite of their manager, working against their boss's wishes to resist. You can see the kind of difficult and awkward position this puts your Outgrower in.

So, if you have managers, focus the majority of your "buy-in energy" on them. Help them understand why you're running Outgrow and their incredibly important role in it. Help them see how their team stacks up against others on your scorecards. Explain the consequences of not participating, such as:

- Their team will not grow while the others do.

- They are actively going against what the company's top leadership is trying to accomplish (intentional organic growth).

This can fall on a continuum between quiet avoidance and active undermining of your work to grow your business.

- They are not leading their group, and likely causing damage to their own advancement opportunities within the organization.

- They are negatively affecting their team's opportunity to take home more money for their families. For salespeople who are compensated on commission, running Outgrow is a fast and easy way to make more money. If their manager is not facilitating their team's implementation of Outgrow—or worse, actively discouraging it—they are intentionally hurting their staff's take-home pay.

Outgrowers Who Don't Understand What to Do

Another common occurrence is staff members who have been trained in Outgrow actions, perhaps more than once, who remain unclear on what to do. Because this kind of proactive outreach, and especially the tracking of it, is new to most customer-facing professionals, some people find it challenging to grasp what's expected of them.

As a result, they might do and log things incorrectly. As I pointed out in the beginning of this chapter, this is almost always an honest misunderstanding. Ask your managers to work with the individuals who appear to be logging reactive work or writing too much or too little in the **Notes** field on the Outgrow Tracking Form. If your managers are not clear on the work, perhaps you can spend some time with them until it becomes clearer.

I encourage you to start with assuming everyone means well and is trying to do things correctly. If they prove you wrong, then you can pull some different, sterner levers. Until then, just work on helping people understand the simple work you are asking them to do. This is usually enough.

A Common Concern: What If They Make It Up?

This is a question I hear during initial discussions with owners and top executives. *What if they just make it up and write down things that didn't happen?* My answer is always to review the notes in the **Actions, Opportunities & Follow-Up** field.

If they write down "had lunch" or "had call" or "met" and nothing more, you can ask some questions about this interaction. But if they write down a line or two with the DYK, rDYK, and opportunity details, then you can rest assured things happened as recorded. Frankly, over hundreds of Outgrow implementations, and easily more than 10,000 individual participants, I can't think of more than two individuals who were found to be recording things that did not happen, which makes it so rare that it's not worth worrying about.

INCENTIVES

The topic of incentives frequently comes up with Outgrow leaders, so I'd like to address it somewhat briefly here. Why briefly? Because it's a topic that's extremely unique and specific to each individual firm. Your own sales compensation history, beliefs, approaches, and current situation all play into how incentives are set up at your organization.

Some Outgrow organizations limit the incentives to the public internal recognition sharing laid out in chapter 7. But many roll out some kind of incentive program to help motivate participation, ranging from gift cards to additional financial compensation. Here are some guidelines:

- **Incentivize Actions, Not Results:** Since Outgrow revolves around counting and recognizing swings of the bat, rather than hits or runs driven in, incentives should be based on efforts as well. You can set minimum requirements of actions for compensations and reward people for their participation.

Repeating from earlier in the book: we incentivize swings because we know the batting averages, and we know that in sales, more swings will *always* lead to more hits. Count the hits if you wish—and you likely have systems that already do—but incentivize and reward the swings.

- **Think About Rewarding Teams, Not Individuals:** A powerful way to encourage participation is to reward everyone on a team or no one. So, if the team averages a certain number of actions per person, per week, each member of the team attains the incentive. The incentive can be financial, a gift card, or lunch on you. The lunch can be earned for the entire office or location, and include people who aren't even participating in Outgrow— say, office staff, production workers, or warehouse staff. It's a reward for many, earned by some, by actively taking action to intentionally grow your sales. Rewarding the team based on the group effort creates an awareness among the group of who is and is not participating, and emphasizes that teamwork—and, yes, sometimes peer pressure—is helpful to our cause.

- **Promotions and Advancement:** Some of my Outgrow clients will simply not promote a staff member if they do not meet a minimum action count per week, over time. Because Outgrow is based entirely on behaviors that people control, some leaders see participation as an indication of caring about growth and the company. And if a person is up for a promotion but shows you they don't care enough to take simple actions to develop business, is that somebody you want at the next level of your company?

OUTGROW SUPPORT RESOURCES

Certified Outgrow Advisors

You now know all of the components of the Outgrow program. You can do it all yourself. Head to RunOutgrow.com for available free tools, and to learn about the various options there to help you with implementing Outgrow at your company. You can sign up for self-implementation guidance, which will give you access to the Outgrow Tracking Form, scorecards, and detailed instructions and videos on how to implement this at your company. And you can also learn about the simple process of hiring a certified Outgrow Advisor to work with you and your team to help you implement this work. If you feel you don't have the capacity or expertise to implement this work—or simply need a helping hand—there are talented, experienced Advisors ready to help!

Chapter 10

RUN OUTGROW!

ere is how to begin running Outgrow at your organization. There are six steps to prepare your Outgrow program, and then two processes to run once you launch.

BUILDING YOUR OUTGROW PROGRAM

First, build your Outgrow program. Involve your Outgrow Implementation Leader here, as well as other company leaders. Take these steps together with your core leadership team, if possible.

First, interview some happy customers: Set up some 20-minute conversations, following the structure laid out in chapter 2. Record the calls and capture from your highly satisfied customers what they are most pleased with and how those things help them.

Next, select your participants: Which customer-facing staff will be involved? Ideally, include all salespeople, customer service people, counter people, and even potentially service providers and delivery drivers.

Create your customer lists: Review the suggested customer and prospect categories in chapter 4 and piece together your customer lists. These will be assigned to your customer-facing people and serve as your starting point for who to proactively call and attempt to help more.

Prepare your Wallet Share Expansion kit: Create lists of product and service offerings for your team to have in front of their eyes. Also, create Wallet Share Expansion plans for your top 10 to 20 customers, considering if there are products or services they are buying today that they can increase their volume on, which additional products they can buy, and if they may have additional buyers of what you sell in their company.

Review the communications with your team: Meet with your team to go over the different kinds of proactive calls and the revenue-growing communications like DYKs, rDYKs, quote and proposal follow-ups, and pivots to the sale.

Prepare your Outgrow Tracking Form: Create your form modeled on the Outgrow Tracking Form in your own CRM or use ours via one of the programs found at RunOutgrow.com.

NOW, RUN OUTGROW

Now that you've built your Outgrow program, it's time to run Outgrow!

Start Your Process:

1. Assign your target actions for Week 1.

2. Your people will go and do the work.

3. They will log the actions.

4. You will output scorecards and data.

5. You will share their success stories weekly.

Run the Outgrow Meetings:

1. Give daily encouragement.

2. Have Weekly Huddles.

3. Do one-on-one Monthly Reviews.

4. Do Outgrow Quarterly Planning.

Congratulations, you are running Outgrow. Enjoy the systematic, predictable growth to come!

RUN OUTGROW
AT YOUR COMPANY

If you'd like some help running Outgrow, I have four options for you. Visit RunOutgrow.com for details on these four options, and more:

HIRE A CERTIFIED OUTGROW ADVISOR

If you are a small- to mid-sized firm, licensed and certified Outgrow Advisors (OAs) are available to guide, consult, and help your organization through the process of changing mindsets and developing a positive, enthusiastic, confident, and bold culture at your organization. They will help you implement the technology tools to effectively run Outgrow and mold, shape, and customize the program specifically to your company's needs. With a mix of in-person training sessions for your team and web-based live sessions, an Outgrow Advisor will ensure your firm achieves the predictable organic growth it deserves.

OUTGROW FOR SALESPEOPLE

If you are an individual salesperson and wish to implement Outgrow proactive growth tactics in your work, but your company is not running the program, you may participate in Outgrow for Salespeople. You will join a small peer group of sales professionals and create systematic organic growth together. You'll receive accountability led by an Outgrow Advisor, and there will be scorecards and success sharing within the group. Many individual salespeople have doubled and sometimes tripled their personal sales with Outgrow.

OUTGROW SOLO

Here is some more good news for solo consultants and providers: there is an Outgrow experience just for you. It's designed to give you the same accountability, planning, and communications rhythms as the corporate teams that run the system. You will work in small teams of other solo providers, and your implementation will be by a licensed Outgrow Advisor. You'll join a cohort of fellow Outgrow Solo participants so that you will enjoy assured, predictable, and *calming* revenue growth.

OUTGROW SMALL BUSINESS

What if you have more than one person working at your company, but the firm generates less than $1M in revenue? We have built a program to help you get to seven figures: it's called Outgrow Small Business and focuses on your unique business development issues and challenges. These are: (1) managing the operational and sales sides of your business, and (2) likely having just one or two people focused on sales, at least one of whom (probably you!) runs the business. Join us, and immerse yourself into Outgrow proactive revenue growth with like-minded business owners interested in fast sales expansion.

Visit www.RunOutgrow.com for details on these Outgrow programs.

ACKNOWLEDGMENTS

This is my seventh commercially published book, and my sixth business book. My very first business book was published by a Dallas outfit called BenBella Books in 2011, which took a chance on a young, inexperienced, hungry author trying to write a business book to help his fledgling consulting company. My kids were newborns when I was shopping that book around, and after hitting the market, it didn't do particularly well. Another publisher, John Wiley & Sons, handled my next four books, and three of them became *Wall Street Journal* bestsellers. In March of 2020, as Covid stormed in, Wiley's executive publisher, Matt Holt (he ran the place), decided to transition out to a new publisher. He started his own imprint, called Matt Holt Books, for . . . a Dallas outfit called BenBella Books. Matt and I met for lunch at a little Nashville bar in the summer of 2023, and committed to work together in the near future. Several months later, *Outgrow* was born. Thank you, Matt, for your trust and belief—it's an honor to work on a book directly with you. And a huge thanks to Glenn Yeffeth, CEO and publisher of BenBella Books, for taking a second chance on a now graying, much more experienced, but equally hungry consultant and author. I am grateful to be with you again. Life comes full circle.

I'd like to also thank my editor and fellow bourbon aficionado Katie Dickman for her focus, help, responsiveness, and guidance on this book. The BenBella team of Brigid Pearson (who designed the excellent cover), Michael Fedison (who handled the copy editing), Jessika Rieck (the production director keeping us on track), and Mallory Hyde Hickok (who oversees the marketing) has been extraordinarily attentive, impressively detail-oriented, and consistently committed to the success of this book.

It's difficult to express how much help and support an entrepreneur and author requires at home, but at our home it runs even deeper: during the difficult times in my business journey, on multiple occasions, my wife, Lisa, believed in my work more than I did. She has encouraged, cheered, motivated, improved, expanded (but also frequently focused), and gracefully guided my work. Our son, Noah, is an entrepreneur in the making, moving through the world with passion, creativity, and a positive energy that impresses everyone he meets. He will be a leader and a business grower. Our daughter, Bella, is an analytic, carefully observing and considering the details before making thoughtful decisions. She also consistently wows audiences with her speaking skills whenever she chooses to break them out. She will be a leader as well, setting an example for everyone around her to follow. I thank my lucky stars for these three wonderful human beings every day.

As anyone who has seen me speak knows, my parents brought me to America from the former Soviet Union when I was two years old. I am grateful to live and work *here*, even when things are challenging, perhaps *especially* when they are challenging. Thank you, Mom and Dad, for taking such immense risks to get us to this incredible country where hard work and perseverance are the answer to all problems. My 97-year-old grandmother, also named Bella, was instrumental in developing my love for the United States. "For America we must pray," she'd announce randomly and frequently, in Russian, whenever something good happened. When I was young and stressed and unsuccessful, she told me I would be okay. "Everything will turn out well. This is America." She was right.

Thanks to Ron, Jan, and Keith Lobodzinski for being wonderful family, always supportive and encouraging, which I appreciate tremendously. During my early days in business, Ron gave valuable advice on important matters, and it helped greatly. I appreciate them always.

Greg, Jeannie, and Sean Livelsberger are neighbors turned friends, turned family that we chose, turned business partners; and we are immensely grateful to have them so close to us.

Lisa and I and the kids are lucky to have our dear friends Ben, Kendall, Myles, and Ainsley Haight; Ben, Karina, Alessandra, and Kathan DeHayes; Jeff, Tara, Cooper, and Eli Zuerlein; and Josh, Jill, Adeline, and Isaac Blacksmith in our lives. We get to spend our quality time with these wonderful families. They are our closest humans, and we're not sure what we did to deserve them.

In my consulting business, I work closest with my executive administrator, Shayla Pitts, who handles the countless details of our busy and expansive consulting practice. She has no trouble keeping up with my fast pace, and learns and adjusts to new projects and initiatives as quickly as I roll them out. She's also a special person who overcomes difficulties with grace and positivity. I am grateful to work with her.

These next three gentlemen are my best friends in business, and each of them knew me when I was young and broke. Each of them helped me when I was working really hard but not succeeding. They've seen my business journey up close, across two decades now, and I appreciate and value them greatly. Wes Trochlil has earned (and receives daily) my tremendous patience during our daily banter. Chris Patterson is the kindest, most caring person I've ever met in business, and Lisa and I love him, Marnie, and their entire family. Jeff Conroy is a tremendous example to me of the amazing things that can be accomplished when we stretch *and* commit ourselves beyond what we're comfortable with. All three have helped my family repeatedly, for as long as I can remember. Personally and professionally, I appreciate these men beyond words.

One day in the fall of 2023, I was keynoting a large executive conference in Tempe, Arizona, for Rick Johnson's Arizona Growth Advisors. I am lucky that in the audience that day was Mari Tautimes, who has had a great impact on my work ever since. Thank you for all your help and energy for helping to get Outgrow LLC off to such a strong start, Mari!

Melissa Smith is a gifted operational organizer and implementer. She makes things run smoothly at Outgrow LLC, managing and delivering support for me, our business, and all of the Outgrow Advisors.

I'd like to thank the following clients for their friendship and support over the years. I've worked closely with all of them for many years now, and they have *each*, in their own unique ways, advanced the Outgrow program forward. They've broken new ground in their application of the proactive growth work at their companies, and have kindly allowed me to incorporate their advancements to future clients. They are the best business leaders I've ever worked with. I learn from them on a regular basis. They have all been to my home multiple times, they know Lisa, and they've watched our kids grow up. Through my Revenue Growth Leaders Client Peer Group, they all know each other also. They are: Paul VanDuyne, Paul Kennedy, Mike Meiresonne, Karl Hallstrom, KayCee Hallstrom, Ryan Hilsinger, Patrick Maloney, Michael Maloney, and Kevin McDonough. I am tremendously grateful for our partnership.

I also want to thank my exceptional clients, nearly all of whom are widely acknowledged as leaders in their respective industries: Steve Jones, Brent Jones, John Wimberly, Shane Kirby, Rob Davidson, Chris Fairchild, Hinesh Patel, Inga Carus, Bruce Hasselbring, Matt Hasselbring, Cindy Motzko, Andrew Matthews, Don Maloney, A. J. Maloney, Mike Zorich, Christy Maloney, Dave Heckler, Wilson Teachey, Will Simpson, Daniel Hart, Danny Davies, Chad Cillessen, Carl Parker, Jeff New, Jordan New, Dan New, Mike Adelizzi, Mike Miazga, Rick Johnson, Tony Hutti, Derek Hutchinson, Finlay Cumming, Stephen Coulthard, Nick Porter, Chris Semerau, Andy Schurman, Gus Childs, Neil Morgan, Matt Brainerd, Dale Harper, Doug O'Rourke, Rob Brown, Stacey Herschberger, Erol Deren, and Scott Hilton. Thank you for your trust and support.

INDEX

ABOUT THE AUTHOR

Alex Goldfayn developed the Outgrow selling system while consulting hundreds of organizations in business-to-business markets like manufacturing, wholesale distribution, and professional service firms. Most of Alex's clients are complex organizations in mature industries, and are either multigenerational family businesses or, more and more, private-equity owned. He does this consulting work as CEO of The Revenue Growth Consultancy, and is the founder of Outgrow LLC.

Alex's three most recent books preceding this one are *Wall Street Journal* bestsellers: *Pick Up the Phone and Sell* (published by Wiley in September 2021), *5-Minute Selling* (Wiley, August 2020), and *Selling Boldly* (Wiley, 2018). His 2015 book, *The Revenue Growth Habit*, was honored as the sales book of the year by 800-CEO-Read, and *Evangelist Marketing* was published in 2012 by BenBella Books.

Alex works in industries like plumbing, HVAC, lumber, chemicals, steel, cartons, engineering, consulting, automation, printing, and many other sexy categories. Most firms have seen flat organic growth or experienced inflationary or acquisitive growth for several years when they come to Alex. They all grow quickly—averaging 20% to 30% annual sales growth. Some add 50% new sales. Many salespeople routinely double and triple their personal sales by applying Alex's approaches.

Alex's speaking work is represented by the Washington Speakers Bureau, and he is one of the highest-rated and most sought-after sales speakers in the world. He frequently keynotes executive conferences, as well as motivating outside and inside sales teams, customer service groups, managers, and other leaders. Alex teaches the Outgrow approaches in his speaking work: simple but powerful mindset shifts (from fear to confidence; from selling to helping) and behaviors (proactively calling customers and prospects when nothing is wrong), which lead to predictable and dramatic revenue growth.

Not only does Alex regularly implement the systems in this book; he applies the approaches in his own firm, one of the highest-grossing and most successful solo consulting practices of any kind.

Alex lives in the Chicago area with his wife, Lisa; 15-year-old twins Noah and Bella; and four—yes, four—doodle dogs.